Why Am I Afraid to Tell You Who I Am?

Insights on self-awareness, personal growth and interpersonal communication

John Powell

Fount

An Imprint of HarperCollins*Publishers*

Fount Paperbacks is an imprint of
HarperCollins*Religious*
Part of HarperCollins*Publishers*
77–85 Fulham Palace Road, London W6 8JB

First published in the U.S.A. in 1967 by
Argus Communications, Illinois
First published in Great Britain in 1975 by Fontana
Reissued in 1978 by Fount Paperbacks
This edition published by Fount in 1995
15 17 19 20 18 16 14

Copyright © 1969 by Argus Communications

John Powell asserts the moral right to be
identified as the author of this work

A catalogue record for this book
is available from the British Library

ISBN 0 00 627849-3

Printed and bound in Great Britain by
Woolnough Bookbinding Ltd, Irthlingborough, Northamptonshire

Contents

1

Understanding the Human Condition

'How beautiful, how grand and liberating this experience is, when people learn to help each other. It is impossible to over-emphasize the imense need humans have to be really listened to, to be taken seriously, to be understood.

'Modern psychology has brought it very much to our attention. At the very heart of all psychotherapy is this type of relationship in which one can tell everything, just as a little child will tell all to his mother.

'No one can develop freely in this world and find a full life without feeling understood by at least one person . . .

'He who would see himself clearly must open up to a confidant freely chosen and worthy of such trust.

'Listen to all the conversations of our world, between nations as well as those between couples. They are for the most part dialogues of the deaf.'

Paul Tourniet, M.D. Swiss Psychiatrist and Author

Then the Lord God said:
'It is not good for man to
be alone . . .'

(Genesis 2:18)

Our word **communication** refers to a process by which someone or something is made common, that is, it is shared. If you tell me a secret, then you and I possess the knowledge of your secret in common, and you have communicated it to me.

But you have much more to communicate to me, if you wish to, than merely one of your secrets. You can tell me who you are, just as I can tell you who I am.

The 'real' person

In our society today, we have placed a great stress on being authentic. We have talked about placing masks over the face of our 'real' selves, and of playing roles which disguise our true and real selves. The implication is that somewhere, inside of you and inside of me, lurk our real selves. Supposedly, this real self is a static and formed reality. There are moments when this real self of mine shines out of me, and there are other moments when I feel compelled to camouflage my real self.

There is perhaps some justification for this manner of speaking, but I think that it can be more misleading than helpful. There is no fixed, true and real person inside of you or me, precisely because **being a person** necessarily implies **becoming a person, being in process**. If I am anything as a person, it is what I

> think
> judge
> feel
> value
> honour
> esteem
> love
> hate
> fear
> desire
> hope for
> believe in
> and
> am committed to.

These are the things that define my person, and they are constantly in process, in the process of change. Unless my mind and heart are hopelessly barricaded, all these things that define me as a person are forever changing.

My person is not a little hard core inside of me, a little fully-formed statue that is real and authentic, permanent and fixed; person rather implies a dynamic process. In other words, if you knew me yesterday, please do not think that it is the same person that you are meeting today.

I have experienced more of life, I have encountered new depths in those I love, I have suffered and prayed, and I am different.

Please do not give me a 'batting average', fixed and irrevocable, because I am 'in there' constantly, taking my swings at the opportunities of daily living. Approach me, then, with a sense of wonder, study my face and hands and voice for the signs of change; for it is certain that I have changed. But even if you recognize this, I may be somewhat afraid to tell you who I am.

The Human Condition

Consider the following conversation:

Author: 'I am writing a booklet, to be called, *Why Am I Afraid to Tell You Who I Am?*'

Other: 'Do you want an answer to your question?'

If I expose my nakedness
as a person to you —
Do not make me feel shame.

Author: 'That is the purpose of the booklet, to answer the question.'

Other: 'But do you want *my* answer?'

Author: 'Yes, of course I do.'

Other: 'I am afraid to tell you who I am, because, if I tell you who I am, you may not like who I am, and it's all that I have.'

This short excerpt was taken from an actual conversation, unrehearsed and from life as it really is. It reflects something of the imprisoning fears and self-doubt which cripple most of us and keep us from forward movement on the road to maturity, happiness, and true love.

In a previous effort, entitled *Why Am I Afraid to Love?*, I have tried to describe something of the human scars and pains which block the way to true love. They are the same scars, the same inner fears and pains, which block the way to true self-communication, on which love is built. Since that other booklet, to which this is intended to be a sequel, is still available, there is no need here to review the psychological dilemmas and distress which are a part of the human condition.

Nevertheless, as a progression from that earlier booklet, we do want to describe here something of how these scars and the defences, which we use to protect ourselves from further vulnerability, tend to form patterns of action and reaction. These patterns eventually become so self-deceptive that we forfeit all sense of identity and integrity. We act 'roles', wear 'masks' and play 'games'.

None of us wants to be a fraud or to live a lie; none of us wants to be a sham, a phoney, but the fears that we experience and the risks that honest self-communication would involve seem so intense to us that seeking refuge in our roles, masks and games becomes an almost natural reflex action.

After a while, it may even be quite difficult for us to distinguish between what we really are, at any given moment in our development as persons, and what we pose as being. It is such a universally human problem that we might justifiably call it 'the human condition'.

It is, at least, the condition in which most of us find ourselves and the point of our departure towards growth, integrity and love.

Transactional analysis

The well-known California psychiatrist, Dr Eric Berne, in his best-selling book, *The Games People Play*, speaks of 'transactional analysis', by which he means an analysis of the social transaction when two people meet in a given situation. In such a situation, there is the 'transactional stimulus' (e.g. a sick child asking for a glass of water) and the 'transactional response' (the mother bringing it). Transactional analysis attempts to diagnose the so-called 'ego states' of the interacting persons (the stimulator and the respondent) at the time of the transaction. The supposition of transactional analysis is that, in various interactions, we may well be acting in a different role or ego state.

These ego states can be divided into three categories: the **Parent** (who is superior, protective and who somehow supplies for the inadequacy of the other), the **Adult** (who is adequate in himself and who relates to another adult as to an equal), and the **Child** (who is inadequate, and therefore stands in need of some kind of help and support). None of us remains fixed permanently in any of these ego states, but we may fluctuate from one to another, depending on the situation at hand and our needs of the moment.

For example, the man who can at times function as a **Parent** to his child, or as an **Adult** to his wife or business associates, is also capable of assuming (either consciously or unconsciously) the ego state of a **Child**. While getting ready to escort his wife to the theatre, where he will most probably assume

I can help you to accept and open yourself mostly by accepting and revealing myself to you.

the ego state of a Parent or Adult, he may say impetuously to his wife, 'Mama, will you please find my cuff-links for me?' The Child that is in him is suddenly activated, because of his need of the moment, although he may quickly revert to one of the other ego states, depending on his physical or emotional needs.

It may also happen that the respondent in the example is inclined to avoid any responsibilities, and the Child in the wife may come to the surface. 'Gee whizz, Daddy, if you can't find them, I'm sure that I certainly can't.' The 'vector line' is strictly horizontal in this transaction: Child is relating to Child.

How we are 'programmed' to choose 'ego states'

Clinical experimentation, applying these theories, has operated on the assumption that all of us are capable of these various ego states, and that we have been programmed by our individual, psychological histories to react as Parent, Adult or Child, in given life-situations. This 'programming' is a result of the composite of previous influences in our lives (social programming) and our reaction to them (individual programming). The stimuli of these previous influences and reactions are recorded indelibly inside us.

The human organism carried within itself something like a portable tape recorder, which is always playing softly but insistently inside us. On the tape of this recorder there plays the message of mother or father (or other). Mother may still be saying: 'Nothing is too good for my little Darling. I'll do the dishes and make the beds. You just run along and play, Honey.' If the reaction of 'Honey' was to accept the role of perpetual child, you may see her (supposed by now to be an adult) running right by you some day, on her way to play, still expecting others to do everything for her, and unwilling to take any responsibility.

Or Daddy's thunder may be on the tape recorder: 'You're no damned good, you Louse!' If the child in this case has reacted in a docile manner, when he passes you, he is likely to be sullen, discouraged, and be mumbling to himself: 'I'm no damned good . . . I'm no damned good!'

Social and individual programming tend to crystallize in patterns of action and reaction. These patterns can often be predicted in most of us with high accuracy. Depending on your physical or emotional needs of the moment, we tend to play the same roles, the same 'games'. And the 'game' always follows the 'programme'. If you want to understand the game correctly, it helps you to know the programme.

Programming: who will dominate in the psycho-drama?

Inside each of us, there is a tape recorder which plays the sound track of a psycho-drama which is continually being enacted. On the stage is Parent (or other), the Child-I, and the Adult-I. Mother or Father is delivering a message to the Child-I. The Child is reacting in his own way. When the Adult-I hears the message, and sees the reaction of the Child, he has to step in and corroborate or deny the message. He has to assert himself, because, if he doesn't, the future of the person involved will be nothing more than a living out of the programming of the past.

For example, if the Parent is saying: 'You'll never amount to anything', the Adult has to step in and reprimand the Parent. 'Stop telling this child that he is no good!' The balance can and has to be tipped. Life has to be more than simply a living out of the programming of the past, and it can be if the Adult in us will intervene.

'But, if I tell you who I am,
you may not like who I am,
and it is all that I have.'

When we speak or act, sometimes the mother or father in us is speaking (the message is indelible and always operative), sometimes the Child-I in us is speaking, and sometimes it is the Adult-I. There are times, too, that the Parent in us interrupts the Child-I, as, for example: 'It is such a nice day outside and I would like to go out and play (Child), but you can't always be doing what you want to (Parent).' At this point the intervening Adult may assert himself and decide: 'But I need some fresh air and I need it now, so I'm going out.'

In other words, there is in each of us not only a variety of ego states, but also an **acculturated self** and a **deliberated self**. This distinction essentially means the same thing as the distinction between the programmed self and the intervening Adult self. The culture or sub-culture in which we live is one of the sources of our programming. It sets us up to react to certain situations in certain ways. When we oblige others with the expected reactions, or we fall into patterns that have been pretty much determined by our past, it is the **acculturated self** which is acting. As a person becomes more and more adult (mature) the **deliberated self**, which acts out of personal integration and conviction, takes over. The fully human being gradually extricates himself from his programming and turns from being a 'reactor' into an 'actor'. He becomes 'his own man (woman)'.

Resorting to games

'Games' in this context are not really fun. They are the patterned reactions to life-situations, programmed for us somewhere back in our personal, psychological history. Sometimes these games are extremely grim affairs, because everyone is playing to win . . . to win something. In order to achieve the honest communication of ourselves to others, to experience the reality of others, to become integrated and to grow, it helps very much to be aware of our patterned reactions — the games we play. If we become aware of these games, we may give them up.

These games are almost always little manoeuvres on our part, which we employ to avoid self-realization and self-communication. They are little shields which we carry in front of us as we enter the battle of life; they are designed to protect us from being hurt and help us to win some little trophy for our egos. Eric Berne calls these little gains 'strokes', little victories or successes which bring us protection or recognition. The games are various because psychological histories and programming are always unique, and because there is a variety of ego states in which we may choose to cast ourselves, depending on the needs of the moment and the life-situation.

The one thing that all of these games have in common is this: They defeat self-knowledge and destroy all possibility of honest self-communication with others. The price of victory is costly; there is little chance for such a person to experience true interpersonal encounters, which alone can put him on the path to human growth and the fullness of human life.

Most of us play games with others in our habitual behaviour. We set others up to react to us in the way that we want them to react. For example, we may not ever grow into authentic persons because we have settled for being children, inadequate and in need. We send out our 'pity signals' in the sound of our voices and in the expressions on our faces. We condition others to react very gently to us. We sound and look as helpless as any child; most people are obliging enough to follow our stage directions.

Others of us, who are messianic in our assumed role, insist on wanting to save others at all times. We want to be 'the helper' and to make everyone else to whom we relate 'the helped'. Sometimes the perpetual child marries the messiah, and they make a lifelong game of it together. Since these two games mesh, things will go very well, and neither of them will ever have to grow up.

If only our fears and insecurity, which prompt us to assume various ego states and play various games, would allow us to be in honest touch with our emotions and able to report them honestly, the patterns of 'pity signals' or 'messianic mystique' would emerge and become obvious to us.

The perpetual child would find that he never relates well to others except when he is bringing his problems and helplessness to them; the self-styled saviour would discover that he never relates well to others unless the other is troubled and helpless . . . and needing him. Being honest with one's self in this way is no easy matter, because it involves letting one's repressed emotions rise to recognition for what they really are; it demands reporting these emotions to others, as we shall see later.

It is doubtful that there is anyone who does not play these or other games. Therefore, if I really want to 'see it like it is . . . and tell it like it is', I must ask myself some difficult questions about the patterns of action and reaction that emerge in my conduct, and I must ask myself what these patterns reveal to me about myself.

Do I subconsciously develop problems in order to get attention? Do I insist on relegating all those

I can only know that much of myself which I have had the courage to confide to you.

with whom I relate to the category of 'those who need my help'? Do I present myself as delicate in order to ensure gentle treatment from others? Am I using other people as conquests to provide a transfusion of life for my limping ego? Am I seeking to impress others with my self-sufficiency, precisely because I doubt my adequacy as a person?

The final section of this booklet is a partial listing of some of the more common roles that people assume for either permanent or occasional use. It could be called a 'catalogue of games and roles'. This section of the booklet, however, is not intended at all to be the 'entertainment' section. All of us experience the 'human condition' of fear and hiding. We all know something of what was meant by: 'But if I tell you who I am, you may not like who I am, and it is all that I have.'

What you and I really need is a moment of truth and a habit of truth with ourselves. We have to ask ourselves in the quiet, personal privacy of our own minds and hearts: What games do I play? What is it that I am trying to hide? What is it that I hope to win?

My willingness to be honest with myself and these questions will be the decisive factor and the essential condition for growth as a person.

A growing person is
self-renewing . . .
as new as each new day . . .
Study his face and hands,
listen to his voice . . .
look for change . . .
it is certain that he
has changed.

2

Growing as a Person

In these pages there are frequent references to 'growth as a person', and much will be said about the necessity of self-communication and interpersonal encounter as means to this growth. It is both intriguing and difficult to try to describe what this 'growth' implies. It is impossible to cite an example of the full-grown person because each of us has to grow into his own person, not become 'like' anyone else.

What kind of person are we trying to become? Carl Rogers calls this person 'the fully functioning person' (*Psychotherapy: Theory, Research and Practice,* 1963), and certainly, since becoming a person is a lifelong, dynamic process, growth will have to be defined largely in terms of functions. Abraham Maslow, the famous psychologist from Brandeis University, calls this person 'the self-actualizing person', and the 'fully-human person'.

Interiority and exteriority

The fully human person preserves a balance between 'interiority' and 'exteriority'.

Both the extreme introvert and the extreme extrovert are off balance. The introvert is almost exclusively concerned with himself; he becomes the centre of gravity in his own universe. Because of his preoccupation with self, he is distracted from the vast world outside. The extreme extrovert pours himself out, moves from one external distraction to another. His life is not reflective at all, and consequently there is little interior deepening. As Socrates said, 'The unreflected life isn't worth living'. The first condition of growth is balance.

'Interiority' implies that a person has explored himself and has experienced himself.

He is aware of the vitality of his senses, emotions, mind and will, and he is neither a stranger to, nor afraid of, the activities of his body and emotions. His senses bring him both beauty and pain, and he refuses neither. He is capable of the whole human gamut of emotions: from grief to tenderness. His mind is alive and searching; his will reaches out for an ever greater possession of all that is good and at the same time savours that which is already in his possession. He has listened to himself, and he knows that nothing which he hears is evil or frighte-nening.

'Interiority' implies self-acceptance.

The desired interiority means that this fully functioning, self-actualizing, fully human person is not only aware of physical, psychological and spiritual hungers and activities, but he accepts them as good. He is 'at home' with his body, his tender as well as hostile emotions, his impulses, thoughts and desires.

Not only is he 'at home' with what he has already experienced within himself, but he is open to new sensations, new and deeper emotional reactions, changing thoughts and desires. He accepts his inner condition as forever changing, since growth is change. His ultimate destiny as a human being, that is, what he will become at the end of his life, is delightfully unknown. No human growth patterns can be pre-structured for all. He doesn't ambition to turn out like anyone else, because he is himself; his potential self, newly actualized every day by new experiences, cannot possibly be defined at any one stage of his growth.

He accepts what he is, physically, emotionally

and intellectually. He knows that what he is, as far as it is known to him, is good; he knows that his potential self is even greater. He is, however, realistic about his limitations; he does not dwell in dreams of what he **wants** to be and spend the rest of his life convincing himself that he **is** these things. He has listened to, explored and loved what he actually is. And each new day this experience of himself will be as new as the day itself because he is forever changing, always a new person, revealed in a constantly changing, self-renovating personality. He trusts his own abilities and resources, confident that he can adapt to and cope with all the challenges that his life will present.

This kind of self-acceptance empowers him to live fully and confidently with all that goes on inside him, and he is afraid of nothing that is or could be a part of himself.

'Exteriority' implies that he is open not only to himself within but to his environment from without.

The fully human person is in deep and meaningful contact with the world outside of him. He not only listens to himself, but to the voices of his world. The breadth of his own individual experience is infinitely multiplied through a sensitive empathy with

The greatest kindness I
have to offer you is
always: the truth.

others. He suffers with the suffering, rejoices with the joyful. He is born again in every Springtime, feels the impact of the great mysteries of life: birth, growth, love, suffering, death. His heart skips along with the 'young lovers', and he knows something of the exhilaration that is in them. He also knows the ghetto's philosophy of despair, the loneliness of suffering without relief, and the bell never tolls without tolling in some strange way for him.

'Create in me, O God, a listening heart', the Psalmist prays.

The opposite of this openness is a kind of 'defensiveness', which hears only what it wants to hear, according to its own preconceived structure and bias, which sees only what it wants to see. The defensive person cannot be a growing person because his world is no bigger than himself and the circle of his horizons is closed.

'Exteriority' reaches its peak in the ability to 'give love freely'.

Dr Karl Stern, a psychiatrist of deep insight, has said that the evolution of human growth is an evolution from an **absolute need to be loved** (infancy) towards a **full readiness to give love** (maturity), with all sorts of stages in between. Dr Stern said: 'In our primary state of union (at the beginning of our growth as persons) we are selfish, and I am, of course, not using the word in its usual moral connotation. The infantile self is still **id** (Freud's term for our drives and ambitions) without differentiation of **ego** (that which, in the Freudian system, adapts and harmonizes personal drives with reality); the **id** of the infantile self is all-engulfing without proper awareness of its own borders. The acts of union of the mature personality are **self-less**.'*

The fully human being can go outside of himself, can be committed to a cause; and he does this **freely**. Of course, the fully human being must be free. There are many philanthropists among us who give of their goods or their time addictively or compulsively. There seems to be some driving need that leaves them restless; some guilt and or anxiety that is an obsessive ring in the nose, leading these people from one good deed to another. The fully human being goes out to others and to God Himself, not by a kind of compulsive-obsessive neurosis, but actively and freely, and simply because he has chosen to do so.

The philosopher Martin Heidegger, in discussing the unions of love, points out two pitfalls which can stifle human growth: a complacent satisfaction

* Institute of Man Symposium on **Neurosis and Personal Growth**, Duquesne University, Pittsburgh, Pa., November 18, 1966.

which settles for that which already is, and, at the other extreme, a restless activity which goes from distraction to distraction in search of something beyond. The result, says Heidegger, is always self-estrangement. In love we must possess and savour that which is, and simultaneously be reaching out to possess (to love) the good more fully. This is the balance achieved by the fully human being between 'what is' and 'what is to come'.

The fully human being, in his love, does not identify himself with what he loves, as though they were accretions to himself. Gabriel Marcel, in his book, *Being and Having*, laments that our civilization teaches us how to take possesion of things, when it should rather initiate us in the art of letting go, for there is neither freedom nor real life without an apprenticeship in dispossession.

Balanced 'interiority' and 'exteriority' is what is meant by integration of personality.

Human nature, contrary to much that has been implied about it, is basically reasonable. Carl Rogers insists that this is his certain conclusion, based on twenty-five years of work in psychotherapy. Man is not a forest of irrational desires and impulses. If this were so, man would not want to be fully human. We are all of us capable of exaggeration; we can turn too

much inward or outward. We can become slaves to
our sense pleasures without reflection on our peace
of soul or upon our social need to love and to give to
others. Or we can exaggerate by becoming prisoners
of 'intellect', alive only from the neck up.

When man lives fully in all of his faculties, and
harmonizes all of his powers, human nature will
prove constructive and trustworthy. In other words,
as Rogers points out, when man functions freely, his
reactions may be trusted; they will be positive,
forward moving, constructive. This is a great act of
faith in human nature that too few of us ever make: If
a man is truly open to all that he is, and if he functions
freely and fully in all of his powers (senses, emotions,
mind and will), his behaviour will harmonize all the
data of his powers, and will be balanced and realistic.
He will be on the path to growth, and that is the
human destiny of man, not perfection but growth.

Acting v. reacting

**The fully human person is an Actor, not a
Reactor.**
The syndicated columnist Sydney Harris tells the
story of accompanying his friend to a news-stand.

The friend greeted the newsman very courteously, but in return received gruff and discourteous service. Accepting the newspaper which was shoved rudely in his direction, the friend of Harris politely smiled and wished the newsman a nice weekend. As the two friends walked down the street, the columnist asked:

'Does he always treat you so rudely?'

'Yes, unfortunately he does.'

'And are you always so polite and friendly to him?'

'Yes, I am.'

'Why are you so nice and friendly to him when he is so unfriendly to you?'

'Because I don't want **him** to decide how **I'm** going to act.'

The suggestion is that the 'fully human' person is 'his own person', that he does not bend to every wind which blows, that he is not at the mercy of all the pettiness, the meanness, the impatience and anger of others. Atmospheres do not transform him as much as he transforms them.

Most of us, unfortunately, feel like a floating boat at the mercy of the winds and waves. We have no ballast when the winds rage and the waves churn. We say things like: 'He made me so mad.' 'You really get to me.' 'Her remark embarrassed me terribly.' 'This weather really depresses me.' 'This job really bores me.' 'The very sight of him saddens me.'

Note that all these things are **doing something to me and my emotions**. I have nothing to say about my anger, depression, sadness, etc. And, like all men, we are content to blame others, circumstances and bad luck. The fully human person, as Shakespeare puts it in *Julius Caesar*, knows that: 'The fault, dear Brutus, is not with our stars, but with ourselves . . .' We can rise above the dust of daily battle that chokes and blinds so many of us; and this is precisely what is asked of us in the process of growth as a person.

There is nothing implied here that suggests **repression** of emotions or which denies the fullness of life in our senses and emotions. The suggestion is rather of **balance** and **integration** of emotions. In the fully alive human person, there can be no such thing as either deadening or unconditionally surrendering to the senses or emotions.

The fully alive person listens to, is attuned to his senses and emotions, but surrendering to them would imply abdication of intellect and choice, those precise powers which make human beings more than brute animals, though a little less than angels. We will say more of this reconciliation of senses, emotions, intellect and will, under another heading.

your slightest look easily
will enclose me though i have
closed myself as fingers, you
open always petal by petal
myself as spring opens
(touching skilfully,
mysteriously) her
first rose.

e. e. cummings

3
Interpersonal Relationships

Harry Stack Sullivan, one of the more eminent psychiatrists of interpersonal relationships in our times, has propounded the theory that all personal growth, all personal damage and regression, as well as all personal healing and growth, come through our relationship with others. There is a persistent, if uninformed, suspicion in most of us that we can solve our own problems and be the masters of our own ships of life, but the fact of the matter is that by ourselves we can only be consumed by our problems and suffer shipwreck. What I am, at any given moment in the process of my becoming a person, will be determined by my relationships with those who love me or refuse to love me, with those whom I love or refuse to love.

It is certain that a relationship will be **only as good as its communication**. If you and I can honestly tell each other who we are, that is, what we think, judge, feel, value, love, honour and esteem, hate, fear, desire, hope for, believe in and are committed to, then and then only can each of us grow. Then and then alone can each of us be what he really is, say what he really thinks, tell what he really feels, express what he really loves. This is the real meaning of authenticity as a person, that my exterior truly reflects my interior. It means I can be honest in the communication of my person to others. And this I cannot do unless you help me. Unless you help me, I cannot grow, or be happy, or really come alive.

I have to be free and able to say my thoughts to you, to tell you about my judgements and values, to expose to you my fears and frustrations, to admit to you my failures and shames, to share my triumphs, before I can really be sure what it is that I am and can become. I must be able to tell you who I am before I can know who I am. And I must know who I am before I can act truly, that is, in accordance with my true self.

The subject-object relationship versus the 'Encounter'

In the language of existential psychology, 'encounter' describes a special relationship between two persons. It is a communion or communication of persons that has been achieved. One existence is communicating to another existence, one existence sharing with another. Gabriel Marcel calls this relationship an 'ontological communion', a real fusion of two people. To illustrate what this means, Marcel explains that very often our emotions and sympathy do not spring to life at all when we encounter the suffering of others in our daily lives. Somehow, Marcel goes on, I just cannot respond to them; they are just 'not there' for me. But, if we should open a letter from a friend many miles away telling us of some great disaster or sickness, we are at once with that friend, one with him, suffering with him; we are together without any qualification.

In the words of Martin Buber, the Jewish philosopher of interpersonality, it is in the **encounter** that the other individual no longer is a person of impersonality, a 'he' or 'she', but becomes for my 'I' a sensitized, correlative 'Thou'. (See Martin Buber, *I-Thou*, New York, Scribner, Edinburgh, T & T Clark. The other person becomes, in some mysterious and almost indefinable way, a special being in my eyes, a part of my world, and a part of my self. Insofar as it is possible, I enter into the world of his reality and he enters into the world of my reality. There has been some kind of fusion, even though each of us remains his own distinct self. As e. e. cummings writes:

'One's not half two. It's two halves of one.'

My friend of encounter is no longer someone 'out there somewhere' who serves my purpose, or who belongs to my club, or who works with me. Ours is no such subject-object relationship; we have experienced that mysterious but certain communion or togetherness. It is this that the existential psychologists call 'encounter'. And the stuff of which encounter is made is honest communication.

Where true encounter exists, and we are saying that it is absolutely essential for growth as a person, the concern of the persons in such an encounter is not so much with the problems and their solutions as with communion, sharing. I open myself and my world to you for your entry, and you open yourself and your world for me to enter. I have allowed you to experience me as a person, in the fullness of my person, and I have experienced you in this way. And for this, I must tell you who I am and you must tell me the same about yourself. Communication is the only avenue to communion.

This is why psychologists such as Erich Fromm say that we cannot love anyone without loving everyone more. If I can communicate with you and you with me only on a 'subject-object' level, we will probably both communicate with others, and even with God

Himself, on this same level. We will remain isolated subjects; others and God will remain merely 'objects' in our world, but not experiences. Unless a person has been opened up by such an encounter, he will have so-called friendships, and will perhaps retain a so-called religious faith (a kind of relationship with God), mostly because these are things that are somehow expected of him. These relationships with others will be social amenities and nothing more. There will be no personal meaning in them.

The world of such a person is a world of objects, things to be manipulated, to serve as distractions and sources of pleasure. The possessions of such a person may be beautiful and expensive or they may be common and cheap, but the person will be lonely. He will come to the end of his life without ever having lived. The dynamic process of person-hood will become a status thing like debris floating on stagnant waters. When the process of person-hood is stifled, all of life becomes a terrible bore. If the edges of life for a given person are sharp, life can be very painful. There will be need for those artificially induced but short-lived stimuli called 'kicks'. These kicks are little attempts to run away from life, short 'trips' in an effort to escape the inexorable intrusion of reality and the essential loneliness of the person without true friends.

Human life has its laws, one of which is: We must **use** things and **love** people. The person whose whole life is lived on the subject-object level, finds that he loves things and uses people. It is the death warrant for happiness and human fulfilment.

Interpersonal Encounter and the Five Levels of Communication

Someone has aptly distinguished five levels of communication on which persons can relate to one another. Perhaps it will help our understanding of these levels to visualize a person locked inside a prison. It is the human being, urged by an inner insistence to go out to others and yet afraid to do so. The five levels of communication, which will be described a little later, represent five degrees of willingness to go outside of himself, to communicate himself to others.

The man in the prison — and he is Everyman — has been there for years, although ironically the grated iron doors are not locked. He can go out of his prison, but in his long detention he has learned to fear the possible dangers that he might encounter. He has come to feel some sort of safety and protection behind the walls of his prison, where he is a voluntary captive. The darkness of his prison even shields him from a clear view of himself, and he is not sure what he would look like in broad daylight. Above all, he is not sure how the world, which he sees from behind his bars, and the people whom he sees moving about in that world, would receive him. He is fragmented by an almost desperate need for that world and for those people, and, at the same time, by an almost desperate fear of the risks of rejection he would be taking if he ended his isolation.

This prisoner is reminiscent of what Viktor Frankl writes in his book, *Man's Search for Meaning*, about his fellow prisoners in the Nazi concentration camp at Dachau. Some of these prisoners, who yearned so desperately for their freedom, had been held captive so long that, when they were eventually released, they walked out into the sunlight, blinked nervously and then silently walked back into the familiar darkness of the prisons, to which they had been accustomed for such a long time.

This is the visualized, if somewhat dramatic, dilemma that all of us experience at some time in our lives and in the process of becoming persons. Most of us make only a weak response to the invitation of encounter with others and our world because we feel uncomfortable in exposing our nakedness as persons. Some of us are willing only to pretend this

To refuse the invitation
to interpersonal encounter
is to be an isolated dot
in the centre of
a great circle . . . a small
island in a vast ocean.

exodus, while others somehow find the courage to go all the way out to freedom. There are various stages in between. These stages are described below, under the headings of the five levels of communication. The fifth level, to be considered first, represents the least willingness to communicate ourselves to others. The successive, descending levels indicate greater and greater success in the adventure.

Level Five: Cliché Conversation This level represents the weakest response to the human dilemma and the lowest level of self-communication. In fact, there is no communication here at all, unless by accident. On this level, we talk in clichés, such as: 'How are you? . . . How is your family? . . . Where have you been?' We say things like: 'I like your dress very much.' 'I hope we can get together again real soon.' 'It's really good to see you.' In fact, we really mean almost nothing of what we are asking or saying. If the other party were to begin answering our question, 'How are you?' in detail, we would be astounded. Usually and fortunately the other party senses the superficiality and conventionality of our concern and question, and obliges by simply giving the standard answer, 'Just fine, thank you.'

This is the conversation, the noncommunication, of the cocktail party, the club meeting, the neighbourhood laundromat, etc. There is no sharing of persons at all. Everyone remains safely in the isolation of his pretence, sham, sophistication. The whole group seems to gather to be lonely together. it is well summarized in the lyrics of Paul Simon in *Sounds of Silence* used so effectively in the movie, *The Graduate*:

And in the naked night I saw
Ten thousand people, maybe more,
People talking without speaking,
People hearing without listening,
People writing sonds that voices never shared.
No one dared
Disturb the sounds of silence.

Level Four: Reporting the facts about others On this fourth level, we do not step very far outside the prison of our loneliness into real communication because we expose almost nothing of ourselves. We remain contented to tell others what so-and-so has said or done. We offer no personal, self-revelatory commentary on these facts, but simply report them. Just as most of us, at times, hide behind clichés, so we also seek shelter in gossip items, conversation pieces, and little narrations about others. We give nothing of ourselves and invite nothing from others in return.

Level Three: My Ideas and Judgements On this level, there is some communication of my person. I am willing to take this step out of my solitary confinement. I will take the risk of telling you some of my ideas and reveal some of my judgements and decisions. My communication usually remains under a strict censorship, however. As I communicate my ideas, etc., I will be watching you carefully. I want to test the temperature of the water before I leap in. I want to be sure that you will accept me with my ideas, judgements and decisions. If you raise your eyebrow or narrow your eyes, if you yawn or look at your watch, I will probably retreat to safer ground. I will run for the cover of silence, or change the subject of conversation, or worse, I will start to say things I suspect that you want me to say. I will try to be what pleases you.

Someday, perhaps, when I develop the courage and the intensity of desire to grow as a person, I will spill all of the contents of my mind and heart before you. It will be my moment of truth. It may even be that I have already done so, but still you can know only a little about my person, unless I am willing to advance to the next depth-level of self communication.

Level Two: My Feelings (Emotions). 'Gut Level' It might not occur to many of us that, once we have revealed our ideas, judgements and decisions, there is really much more of our persons to share. Actually, the things that most clearly differentiate and individuate me from others, that make the communication of my person a unique knowledge, are my **feelings** or **emotions**.

If I really want you to know who I am, I must tell you about my stomach (gut-level) as well as my head. My ideas, judgements, and decisions are quite conventional. If I am a Republican or Democrat by persuasion, I have a lot of company. If I am for or against space exploration, there will be others who will support me in my conviction. But the **feelings** that lie under my ideas, judgements and convictions are uniquely mine. No one supports a political party, or has a religious conviction, or is committed to a cause with my exact feelings of fervour or apathy. No one experiences my precise sense of frustration, labours under my fears, feels my passions. Nobody opposes war with my particular indignation or supports patriotism with my unique sense of loyalty.

It is these feelings, on this level of communication, which I must share with you, if I am to tell you who I really am. To illustrate this, I would like to put in the left-hand column a judgement, and in the right-hand column some of the possible emotional reactions to this judgement. If I tell you only the contents of my mind, I will be withholding a great deal about myself, especially in those areas where I am uniquely personal, most individual, most deeply myself.

Judgement	Some possible emotional reactions
I think that you are intelligent.	. . . and I am jealous.
	. . . and I feel frustrated.
	. . . and I feel proud to be your friend.
	. . . and it makes me ill at ease with you.
	. . . and I feel suspicious of you.
	. . . and I feel inferior to you.
	. . . and I feel impelled to imitate you.
	. . . and I feel like running away from you.
	. . . and I feel the desire to humiliate you.

Most of us feel that others will not tolerate such emotional honesty in communication. We would rather defend our dishonesty on the grounds that it might hurt others, and, having rationalized our phoneyness into nobility, we settle for superficial

Most people tend to
overcompensate . . .
People who are riddled
with doubts tend to be
dogmatists who are
never wrong!

relationships. This occurs not only in the case of casual acquaintances, but even with members of our own families; it destroys authentic communion within marriages. Consequently, we ourselves do not grow, nor do we help anyone else to grow. Meanwhile we have to live with repressed emotions — a dangerous and self-destructive path to follow. Any relationship, which is to have the nature of true personal encounter, must be based on this honest, open, gut-level communication. The alternative is to remain in my prison, to endure inch-by-inch death as a person.

We will say more of this level of communication, after describing the first and deepest level of communication between persons.

Level One: Peak Communication All deep and authentic friendships, and especially the union of those who are married, must be based on absolute openness and honesty. At times, gut-level communication will be most difficult, but it is at these precise times that it is most necessary. Among close friends or between partners in marriage there will come from time to time a complete emotional and personal communion.

In our human condition this can never be a permanent experience. There should and will be, however, moments when encounter attains perfect communication. At these times the two persons will feel an almost perfect and mutual empathy. I know that my own reactions are shared completely by my friend; my happiness or my grief is perfectly reduplicated in him. We are like two musical instruments playing exactly the same note, filled with and giving forth precisely the same sound. This is what is meant by level one, peak communication. (Cf. A. H. Maslow, *Religions, Values, and Peak Experiences*, 1964).

'Rules' for gut-level communication

If friendship and human love are to mature between any two persons, there must be absolute and honest mutual revelation; this kind of self-revelation can be achieved only through what we have called 'gut-level' communication. There is no other way, and all the reasons which we adduce to rationalize our cover-ups and dishonesty must be seen as delusions. It would be much better for me to tell you how I really feel about you than to enter into the stickiness and discomfort of a phoney relationship.

Dishonesty always has a way of coming back to

haunt and trouble us. Even if I should have to tell you that I do not admire or love you emotionally, it would be much better than trying to deceive you and having to pay the ultimate price of all such deception, your greater hurt and mine. And you will have to tell me things, at times, that will be difficult for you to share. But really you have no choice, and, if I want your friendship, I must be ready to accept you as you are. If either of us comes to the relationship without this determination of mutual honesty and openness, there can be no friendship, no growth; rather there can be only a subject-object kind of thing that is typified by adolescent bickering, pouting, jealousy, anger and accusations.

The classic temptation in this matter, and it would seem to be the most destructive of all delusions in this area of human relations, is this: we are tempted to think that communication of an unfavourable emotional reaction will tend to be decisive. If I tell you that it bothers me when you do something you are accustomed to do, I may be tempted to believe that it would be better not to mention it. Our relationship will be more peaceful. You wouldn't understand, anyway.

So I keep it inside myself, and each time you do your thing my stomach keeps score 2 . . . 3 . . . 4 . . . 5 . . . 6 . . . 7 . . . 8 . . . until one day you do the same thing that you have always done and all hell breaks loose. All the while you were annoying me, I was keeping it inside and somewhere, secretly, learning to hate you. My good thoughts were turning to gall.

When it finally erupted in one great emotional avalanche, you didn't understand. You thought that this kind of reaction was totally uncalled for. The bonds of our love seemed fragile and about to break. And it all started when I said: 'I don't like what she's doing, but it would be better not to say anything. The relationship will be more peaceful.' That was all a delusion, and I should have told you in the beginning. Now there has been an emotional divorce, all because I wanted to keep the peace between us.

Rule one: Gut-level communication (emotional openness and honesty) must never imply a judgement of the other. I am simply not mature enough to enter into true friendship unless I realize that I cannot judge the intention or motivation of another. I must be humble and sane enough to bow before the complexity and mystery of a human being. If I judge you, I have only revealed my own immaturity and ineptness for friendship.

Emotional candour does not ever imply a judgement of you. In fact, it even abstains from any judgement of myself. For example, if I were to say to you,

'I am ill at ease with you', I have been emotionally honest and at the same time have not implied in the least that it is your fault that I am ill at ease with you. Perhaps it is my own inferiority complex or my exaggerated concept of your intelligence. I am not saying it is anyone's fault, but simply giving a report of my emotional reaction to you at this time.

If I were to say to you that I feel angry or hurt by something you have done or said, it remains the same. I have not judged you. Perhaps it is my own self-love that has made me so sensitive, or my inclination to paranoia (a persecution complex). I am not sure, and, in most cases, I can never be sure. To be sure would imply a judgement. I can only say for sure that this has been and is my emotional reaction.

If I were to tell you that something you do annoys me, again I would not be so arrogant as to think that your action would annoy anyone. I do not even mean that your action is in any way wrong or offensive. I simply mean that here and now I experience annoyance. Perhaps it is my headache or digestion or the fact that I did not get much sleep last night. I really do not know. All that I know is this, that I am trying to tell you that I am experiencing annoyance at this moment.

It would probably be most helpful in most cases to preface our gut-level communication with some kind of a disclaimer to assure the other that there is no judgement implied. I might begin by saying, 'I don't know why this bothers me, but it does . . . I guess that I am just hypersensitive, and I really don't mean to imply that it is your fault, but I do feel hurt by what you are saying.'

Of course, the main thing is that there is **in fact** no judgement. If I am in the habit of judging the intentions or motivation of another, I should try very hard to outgrow this adolescent habit. I simply will not be able to disguise my judgements, no matter how many disclaimers I make.

On the other hand, if I am really mature enough to refrain from such judgements, this too will eventually be apparent. If I really want to know the intention or motivation or reaction of another, there is only one way to find out: **I must ask him**. (Don't pass this by lightly. You don't have x-ray eyes either!)

Perhaps a word should be inserted here about the difference between judging a person and judging an action. If I see someone stealing another's money, I can judge that this **action** is morally wrong, but I cannot judge **him**. It is for God, not for you or me, to judge human responsibility. If, however, we could not judge the rightness or wrongness of an action, it would be the end of all objective morality. Let us not fall into this, that there is nothing objectively wrong

To reveal myself openly
and honestly takes
the rawest kind of courage.

or right, that it is all in the way you look at it. But to judge the responsibility of another is playing God.

Rule two: Emotions are not moral (good or bad)

Theoretically, most of us would accept the fact that emotions are neither meritorious nor sinful. Feeling frustrated, or being annoyed, or experiencing fears and anger do not make one a good or a bad person. Practically, however, most of us do not accept in our day-to-day living what we would accept in theory. We exercise a rather strict censorship of our emotions. If our censoring consciences do not approve certain emotions, we repress these emotions into our subconscious mind. Experts in psychosomatic medicine say that the most common cause of fatigue and actual sickness is the repression of emotions. The fact is that there are emotions to which we do not want to admit. We are ashamed of our fears, or we feel guilty because of our anger or emotional-physical desires.

Before anyone can be liberated enough to practise 'gut-level communication', in which he will be emotionally open and honest, he must feel convinced that emotions are **not moral** but simply **factual**. My jealousies, my anger, my sexual desires, my fears, etc., do not make me a good or bad person. Of course, these emotional reactions must be integrated by my mind and will, but before they can be integrated, before I can decide whether I want to act on them or not, I must allow them to arise and I must clearly hear what they are saying to me. I must be able to say, without any sense of moral reprehension, that I am afraid or angry or sexually aroused.

Before I will be free enough to do this, however, I must be convinced that emotions are not moral, neither good nor bad in themselves. I must be convinced, too, that the experience of the whole gamut of emotions is a part of the human condition, the inheritance of every man.

Rule three: Feelings (emotions) must be integrated with the intellect and will It is extremely important to understand this next point. The non-repression of our emotions means that we must experience, recognize and accept our emotions fully. It does not in any way imply that we will always **act on** those emotions. This would be tragic and the worst form of immaturity, if a person were to allow his feelings or emotions to control his life. It is one thing to feel and to admit to myself and to others that I am afraid, but it is another thing to allow this fear to overwhelm me. It is one thing for me to feel and to admit that I am angry and another to punch you in the nose.

Intellect

Will   *Feelings (emotions)*

In the triangle above we see the three faculties of man which must be integrated, that is, brought into one harmonious wholeness, if one is to advance in the process of becoming a person. If the meaning of this integration is clear, it is apparent that the mind judges the necessity of acting upon certain emotions that have been fully experienced, and the will carries this judgement into effect. For example, I may feel a strong fear of telling you the truth in some given matter. The fact is, and it is neither good nor bad in itself, that I am experiencing fear. I allow myself to feel this fear, to recognize it. My mind makes the judgement that I should not act on this fear, but in spite of it, and to tell you the truth. The will consequently carries out the judgement of the mind. I tell you the truth.

However, if I am seeking a real and authentic relationship with you, and wish to practise 'gut-level' communication, I must tell you something like this:

'I really don't know why . . . maybe it's my streak of cowardice . . . but I feel afraid to tell you something, and yet I know that I must be honest with you . . . This is the truth as I see it . . .'

Or, to take another example, maybe I feel very tender and loving towards you. As Chesterton once remarked, the meanest fear of all is the fear of sentiment. Perhaps it is our cultural heritage or maybe it is the fear of rejection, but we often experience a great reluctance to be externally tender and loving. Perhaps in this case my mind will pass the judgement that it is right to act on this impulse of feeling, and again my will carries the judgement into execution. It should be obvious that, in the integrated person, emotions are neither repressed nor do they assume control of the whole person. They are recognized (What is it that I am feeling?) and integrated (Do I want to act on this feeling or not?).

Rule four: In 'gut-level' communication, emotions must be 'reported' If I am to tell you who I really am, I must tell you about my feelings, whether I will act upon them or not. I may tell you that I am angry, explaining the fact of my anger without inferring any judgement of you, and not intending to act upon this anger. I may tell you that I am afraid, explaining the fact of my fear without accusing you of being its cause, and at the same time not succumbing to the fear. But I must, if I am to open myself to you, allow you to experience (encounter) my person and tell you about my anger and my fear.

It has been truly said that we either **speak out** (report) our feelings or we will **act them out**. Feelings are like steam that is gathering inside a kettle. Kept inside and gathering strength, they can blow the human lid off, just as the steam inside the kettle will blow off the lid of the kettle.

We have already referred to the verdict of psychosomatic medicine that repressed emotions are the most common cause of fatigue and actual sickness. This is part of the 'acting out' process. Repressed emotions may find their outlet in the 'acting out' of headaches, skinrashes, allergies, asthma, common colds, aching backs or limbs, but they can also be acted out in the tension of tightened muscles, the slamming of doors, the clenching of fists, the rise of blood pressure, the grinding of teeth, tears, temper tantrums, acts of violence. We do not bury our emotions **dead**; they remain **alive** in our subconscious minds and intestines, to hurt and trouble us. It is not only much more conducive to an authentic relationship to report our true feelings, but it is equally essential to our integrity and health.

The most common reason for not reporting our

emotions is that we do not want to admit to them for one reason or another. We fear that others might not think well of us, or actually reject us, or punish us in some way for our emotional candour. We have been somehow 'programmed' not to accept certain emotions as part of us. We are ashamed of them. Now we can rationalize and say that we cannot report these emotions because they would not be understood, or that reporting them would disturb a peaceful relationship, or evoke an emotionally stormy reaction from the other; but all of our reasons are essentially fraudulent relationships. Anyone who builds a relationship on less than openness and honesty is building on sand. Such a relationship will never stand the test of time, and neither party to the relationship will draw from it any noticeable benefits.

Rule five: With rare exceptions, emotions must be reported at the time that they are being experienced. It is much easier for most of us to report an emotion that is a matter of history. It is almost like talking about another person when I can talk about myself a year or two years ago, and admit that I was very fearful or very angry at that time. Because they were transient emotions and are now gone, it is easy to dissociate these feelings from my person here and now. It is difficult, however, to recapture a feeling once it has passed into my personal history. We are very often puzzled by such previous emotions: 'I don't know why I ever got so excited.' The time to report emotions is the time when they are being experienced. Even temporary deferral of this report of emotions is unwise and unhealthy.

All communication must obviously respect not only the transmitter of the communication but also the receiver who is to accept the communication. Consequently, it could occur that, in the integration of my emotions, my judgement may dictate that this is not the opportune moment to report my emotional reaction. If the receiver is so emotionally disturbed himself that he could hardly be in a receptive mood, and my report would only be distorted somehow by his turbulent emotional state, it may be that I will have to defer this report.

But, if the matter is serious enough and the emotions strong enough, this period of deferment cannot be too long nor can I be frightened or bullied into complete repression of emotions. Note that this period of deferment should never be a long one, and it would seem that in most cases it would be a rare thing.

Also, it would seem to be a valid exception to this rule to defer or eliminate this report in the case of a passing incident with a chance acquaintance. The gruff manner of a bus driver may irk me, without this being the occasion for me to stand nose to nose with him and tell him about my emotional reactions to him. In the case of two people, however, who must work or live together or who want to relate deeply, this emotional reporting at the time of the emotions is vitally important.

The benefits of 'gut-level' communication

The obvious and primary benefit of 'gut-level' communication will be a real and authentic relationship and what we have called a true 'encounter' of persons. Not only will there be mutual communication of persons and the consequent sharing and experiencing of personhood, but it will result in a more and more clearly defined sense of self-identity for each of the parties in the relationship.

Today, many of us are asking: 'Who am I?' It has come to be a socially fashionable question. The implication is that I do not really know my own self as a person. We have said that my person is what I think, judge, feel, etc. If I have communicated these things freely and openly, as clearly as I can and as honestly as I can, I will find a noticeable growth in my own sense of identity as well as a deeper and more authentic knowledge of the other. It has come to be a psychological truism that I will understand only as much of myself as I have been willing to communicate to another.

The second and very important result of such communication is that, having understood myself because I have communicated myself, I will find the patterns of immaturity changing into patterns of maturity. I will change! Anyone who sees the **patterns** of his reactions, and is willing to examine them, may come to the realization that these are patterns of hypersensitivity or paranoia. At the moment the realization penetrates him, he will find the pattern changing. Notwithstanding all that we have said about emotions, we must not believe that emotional patterns are purely biological or inevitable. **I can and will change my emotional patterns**, that is, I will move from one emotion to another, if I have honestly let my emotions arise for recognition and, having honestly reported them, judge them to be immature and undesirable.

For example, if I consistently and honestly report the emotion of 'feeling hurt' by many small and inconsequential things, it will become apparent to me in time that I am hypersensitive and that I have

The behaviour of the
fully human being is
always unpredictable —
simply because it is FREE

been indulging myself in self-pity. The moment that this becomes clear to me, really hits me, I will change.

In summary the dynamic is this: we allow our emotions to arise so that they can be identified; we observe the patterns in our emotional reactions, report and judge them. Having done these things, we instinctively and immediately make the necessary adjustments in the light of our own ideals and hopes for growth. We change. Try this and see for yourself.

As has been said, our emotional reactions are not biological or psychological necessities. We can move from one emotion to another if we want to. So many examples could be added. I can feel viciously competitive, but if I allow the emotions under my spirit of competition to surface for recognition, I may discover that it is only my sense of inferiority, my lack of belief in myself that propels me into competition. It is strangely mysterious how, when these emotions are allowed to illuminate our inner selves, they can tell us things we never knew about ourselves. This kind of self-knowledge is the beginning of growth.

Or I might be labouring with a destructive emotion like despair, which, if I allow it to rise for inspection, will show itself to be merely an attempt at self-punishment. Most 'depression' is simply self-punishment. Further investigations may show me that I have a guilt complex, and that I need this punishment to atone for my guilt-feelings. I am on a course of self-destruction. When I can recognize these emotions as negative and self-destroying, it is then within my power to move to a new emotional reaction, from self-pity or self-punishment to love, from anger to empathy, from despair to hope.

If all this is true, and you have only to experience it to know its truth, it is obvious that the little phrase we have used so conveniently, 'I'm sorry, but that's the way I am', is nothing more than a refuge and delusion. It is handy if you don't want to grow up; but if you do want to grow up, you try to rise above this fallacy.

The third benefit of 'gut-level' communication is that it will evoke from others a responsive honesty and openness, which is necessary if the relationship is to be interpersonal, mutual. Goldbrunner, a psychiatrist, somewhat boastfully claims that he can gain instant access to the deepest parts of anyone within a matter of minutes. His technique is not to begin by probing with questions for this only makes the insecure person more defensive. The theory of this psychiatrist is that if we want another to be open with us, we must begin by opening ourselves to him, by telling the other honestly and openly of our feelings.

Person is resonant to person, Goldbrunner insists. If I am willing to step out of the darkness of my prison, to expose the deepest part of me to another person, the result is almost always automatic and immediate: The other person feels empowered to reveal himself to me. Having heard of my secret and deep feelings, he is given the courage to communicate his own. This, in the last analysis, is what we meant by 'encounter'.

Whatever my secrets
are, remember when I
entrust them to you, they
are part of me

4

Dealing with our Emotions

W e have said that the fully human being does not repress his emotions, as far as this is under his control, but allows them to rise to the surface of recognition. He experiences the fullness of his emotional life; he is 'in touch with', attuned to his emotions, aware of what they are saying to him about his needs and his relationships with others. On the other hand, we have also said that this does not imply surrender to the emotions. In the fully human person, there is a balance of senses, emotions, intellect and will. The emotions have to be integrated. Though it is necessary to 'report' our emotions, it is not at all necessary that we 'act on' them.

The critical importance of all this will be clear to you if you will reflect for just a moment that (1) almost all the pleasures and pains of life are deeply involved with the emotions. (2) Most human conduct is the result of emotional forces (even though we are all tempted to pose as pure intellects, and to explain on rational, objective grounds all of our preferences and actions). (3) Most interpersonal conflicts result from emotional stresses (e.g. anger, jealousy, frustrations, etc.), and most interpersonal encounters are achieved through some kind of emotional communion (e.g. empathy, tenderness, feelings of affection and attraction). In other words, your emotions and how you deal with them will probably make you or break you in the adventure of life.

The mechanics of 'awareness', 'reporting', and 'integration' of the emotions may be illustrated as follows.

Situation: You are having a discussion with a member of your family or a friend. There are several differences of opinion, and very gradually voices and blood pressures rise. You are beginning to feel the stress of strong feelings. What should you do?

Healthy

1) Be aware of your emotions. Turn your mind briefly away from the argument and pay direct attention to your emotional reaction. Ask yourself: What am I feeling? Is it embarrassment (because his arguments sound better)? Is it fear (he is pretty big and getting more angry by the minute)? Superiority (because you're ahead on points and he knows it)?

2) Admit your emotions. Turn your full awareness towards the emotion. Take a good look, so you can identify it. Estimate, too, how strong it is. It is anger, e.g., and it is pretty high voltage, too.

3) Investigate your emotion. If you really want to find out a lot about yourself, ask your anger how it got there, and where it came from. Trace the origin of your emotion. You may not be able to uncover the whole family tree of your present emotion, but you may just get a glimpse of an inferiority complex to which you have never admitted.

Unhealthy

1) Ignore your emotional reaction. It has nothing to do with the argument anyway. Better yet (if you want to make the worst mistake) tell yourself that you're not getting upset at all. If you are perspiring, tell yourself that it's just warm in the room. Keep your anger down in the pit of your stomach, where your head can't notice it. Feeling emotions during an intellectual discussion is unworthy of you anyway.

2) Keep denying your emotions. Tell yourself and tell others 'But I'm not mad at all'. Emotions are more easily ignored if you keep your mind fixedly on the argument. Don't let your emotions distract you. You can take Alka Seltzer later, when your stomach calls you a liar.

3) Keep combing through your mind for rebuttal materials. The guy with the right moves and bright lines is going to break this thing wide open. It's strictly win-lose now. Slow the words down; you're starting to splutter. But keep up a steady flow, or he'll get in there and make his point. Keep your mind on the argument, and keep moving towards the jugular vein.

Healthy

4) Report your emotion. Just the facts now. No interpretations or judgements. 'Let's cool it for a minute. I'm getting too worked up, and I'm starting to say things I really don't mean.' It is very important not to accuse or judge in this report. Do not tell him that it is his fault that you got so angry. It really isn't his fault, you know. It's something in you. Don't blame him even to yourself.

5) Integrate your emotions. Having listened to your emotion, and having questioned it and reported it, now let your mind judge what is the right thing to do, and let your will carry out the judgement, say, e.g., 'Let's start again. I think I've been too defensive to listen to you. I'd like to try again.' Or, 'Would you mind if we dropped the subject? I'm afraid I'm getting too touchy to discuss anything.'

Unhealthy

4) If you should blow your cool completely and become incoherent, blame it on him. And be sure to include some deep personality defect in your indictment. Tell him, e.g., 'It's impossible to discuss anything with you. You're too damned arrogant. You never (generalizations like this are good, too) listen. You think you're God, don't you?' (Make sure he knows that the question is rhetorical.)

5) Since you haven't even admitted to having an emotion, you won't have to go through the trouble of trying to learn from your emotional reactions or integrating them. Repressed emotions, however, have a way of acting up, so walk out in a huff, and take a couple of aspirins — and keep your mind on how unreasonable he was.

Most of us feel that others will not tolerate such emotional honesty in communication. We would rather defend our dishonesty on the grounds that it might hurt others; and, having rationalized our phoneyness into nobility, we settle for superficial relationships

Reflections on 'Estrangement' and 'Encounter'

In spite of our unwillingness and reluctance to tell others who we are, there is in each one of us a deep and driving desire to be understood. It is clear to all of us that we want very badly to be loved, but, when we are not understood by those whose love we need and want, any sort of deep communication becomes a nervous and uncomforting thing. It does not enlarge and enliven us. It becomes clear that no one can really love us effectively unless he really understands us. Anyone who feels that he is understood, however, will certainly feel that he is loved.

If there is no one who understands me, and who accepts me for what I am, I will feel 'estranged'. My talents and possessions will not comfort me at all. Even in the midst of many people, I will always carry within me a feeling of isolation and aloneness. I will experience a kind of 'solitary confinement'. It is a law, as certain as the law of gravity, that he who is understood and loved will grow as a person; he who is estranged will die in his cell of solitary confinement, alone.

There are many things inside every one of us which we would like to share. All of us have our

To tell you my THOUGHTS is to locate myself in a category. To tell you about my FEELINGS is to tell you about ME.

own secret past, our secret shames and broken dreams, our secret hopes. Over and against this need and desire to share these secrets and to be understood, every one of us must weigh fear and risk. Whatever my secrets are, they seem, more than anything else, to be deeply and uniquely a part of me. No one has ever done the precise things that I have done, no one has ever thought my thoughts, or dreamed my dreams. I am not sure that I could even find the words to share these things with another, but what I am even less sure of is this: how would they sound to another?

The person who has a good self-image, who really and truly accepts himself, will be greatly helped at this time of dilemma. It is not very likely, however, that someone, who has never really shared himself, could have the support of a good self-image. Most of us have experienced and done things, have lived with sensations and feelings, that we feel we would never dare tell another. To the other, I might appear deluded or even evil, ridiculous or vain. My whole life could appear as a hideous deceit.

A thousand fears keep us in the solitary confinement of estrangement. In some of us there is the fear of breaking down, of sobbing like a child. Others of us feel restrained by the fear that the other person will not sense the tremendous importance of my secret to me. We usually anticipate how deep the pain would be if my secret were met with apathy, misunderstanding, shock, anger or ridicule. My confidant might become angry or reveal my secret to others for whom it was not intended.

It may have happened that, at some point in my life, I took some part of me out of the darkness and placed it in the light for the eyes of another. It may be that he did not understand, and I ran full of regrets into a painful emotional solitude. Yet, there may have been other moments when someone heard my secret and accepted my confidence in gentle hands. I may remember what he said to assure me, the compassion in his voice, the understanding look in his eyes. I remember what those eyes looked like. I remember how his hand took mine. I remember the gentle pressure that told me that I was understood. It was a great and liberating experience, and, in its wake, I felt so much more alive. An immense need had been answered in me to be really listened to, to be taken seriously, and to be understood.

It is only through this kind of sharing that a person comes to **know himself**. Introspection of itself is helpless. A person can confide all of his secrets to the docile pages of his personal diary, but he can know himself and experience the fullness of life only in the meeting with another person. Friendship becomes a great adventure. There is a continuously deeper discovery of myself and my friend, as we continue to reveal new and keeper layers of ourselves. It opens my mind, widens my horizons, fills me with new awareness, deepens my feelings, gives my life meaning.

Yet the barriers are never permanently broken. Friendship and mutual self-revelation have a newness about them with each new day, because being a human person involves daily change and growth. My friend and I are growing, and differences are becoming more apparent. We are not growing into the same person, but each into his own. I discover in my friend other tastes and preferences, other feelings and hopes, other reactions to new experiences. I discover that this business of telling him who I am cannot be done once and for all. I must **continually** tell you who I am and you must **continually** tell me who you are, because both of us are continually evolving.

It may be that the very things which first attracted me to you now seem to work against communication. In the beginning, your sentiment seemed to balance off my more intellectual inclinations; your extroverted ways complemented my introversion; your realism counter-balanced my artistic intuition. It seemed like such an ideal friendship. We seemed like separate halves that needed each other to become one whole. But now, when I want you to share my intellectual vision, I am annoyed that you take no interest in my objective arguments of reason. Now, when I want to show you that you are not logical in your sentiment, it does not seem to matter to you at all. In the beginning we seemed to fit together so well. Now your desire to go out to others and my more introverted inclinations which seek solitude seem to be divisive.

Of course, our friendship can still be. We are standing within arms' reach of that which is most humanly rewarding and beautiful. We must not turn back now. We can still share all the things we once shared with such excitement, when first I told you who I was and you told me who you were; only now our sharing will be deeper because we are deeper. If I will continue to hear you with the same sense of wonder and joy as I did in the beginning, and you will hear me in this way, our friendship will grow firmer and deeper roots. The tinsel of our first sharing will mellow into gold. We can and will be sure that there is no need to hide anything from each other, that we have shared everything.

I am continually experiencing the ever-growing, ever-new reality of you, and you are experiencing the reality of me, and, through each other, we are together experiencing the reality of God, who once said that '. . . it is not good for man to be alone'.

> *your slightest look*
> *easily will enclose me*
> *though i have closed*
>   *myself as fingers,*
> *you open always petal*
>   *by petal*
> *myself as spring opens*
> *(touching skilfully, mysteriously)*
> *her first rose*
>
>   *e. e. cummings*

The fully human person is in
deep and meaningful contact with
the world outside of him.
He not only listens to himself, but to
the voices of his world. The breadth of his
own individual experience is infinitely
multiplied through a sensitive empathy with
others. He suffers with the suffering, rejoices
with the joyful. He is born again in every
Springtime, feels the impact of the great
mysteries of life: birth, growth, love,
suffering, death. His heart skips along with
the 'young lovers', and he knows something
of the exhilaration that is in them. He also
knows the ghetto's philosophy of despair,
the loneliness of suffering without relief,
and the bell never tolls without tolling
in some strange way for him.

5

Human Hiding Places: Methods of Ego Defence

Reaction formation

Before proceeding to a catalogue of various roles and games, it seems necessary to say something about the methods of ego defence, which are always somehow involved in these roles and games. In brief, these ego defences are compensations cultivated to counterbalance and camouflage something else in us which we consider a defect or a handicap.

The great Alfred Adler first became interested in **compensation** as a psychological phenomenon, when he noticed how human nature tends to make up for bodily deficiencies. One kidney takes over the function of two if one fails to function. The same thing is true of lungs. A bone fracture which heals properly makes the place of the fracture become stronger than normal.

It is also true that many famous people have developed some skill to an extraordinay degree precisely because they were trying to overcome some handicap. Glenn Cunningham, the first of the famous American mile runners, probably became such a great runner trying to strengthen his legs which were seriously crippled at age seven in a fire that almost took his life. Charles Atlas became the first of the famous body-builders because, as an adolescent, his puny physique was such an embarrassment to him. There is also what is called 'vicarious compensation', by which a perosn handicapped in one way learns to excel in another. The famous painter, Whistler, flunked out of West Point and forfeited his desires for a career in the military, but learned to excel as an artist by developing his talents in that field.

The 'reaction formation', which we are considering here, is an overcompensation by exaggerating or overdeveloping certain conscious trends as a defence against unconscious tendencies of an opposite and unapprovable character, which threaten to break into conscious recognition. The extremely dogmatic person, who is absolutely sure of everything, consciously cultivates this posture of certainty because of demoralizing doubts in his subconscious mind. His self-image isn't strong enough to live with these doubts. People who are overly-tender, to the point of exaggerated sentimentality, are usually suspected of assuming this attitude in compensaion for harsh and cruel tendencies which have been repressed into the subconscious mind.

Prudishness, in an extreme form, is usually an over-compensation for repressed normal sexual desires with which the prude cannot live in comfort. The person who seems to exert an exaggerated concern for the health of his aged parent probably does so to compensate for the subconscious desire to be freed of responsibility for that parent by the death of the same.

Please note well that we cannot suspect every good inclination of being a psychological cover-up for opposite inclination. The thing about reaction formation is that it is always an overcompensation, an exaggerated reaction. Compensatory attitudes are a leaning over backwards to avoid tipping forward. This kind of compensation, once set in motion, always results in an exaggeration or extreme. It is, consequently, only exaggerated behaviour of any kind, which is suspect of being compensatory 'reaction formation'. The dogmatist is never wrong. The prude is hyper-chaste. The reformer-type, preachy and self-righteous, viciously hates sin and sinner alike without any recognition of normal human weakness.

The conclusion is this: **exaggerated behaviour** in a person usually means **just the opposite** of what it implies. Very often we accuse the dogmatist of pride and feel 'called' to help him learn sweet humility. In fact, he is not at all sure of himself, and the more we try to defeat him, to cultivate doubts in him and expose his errors, the more he has to compensate. His dogmatism will probably become even more extreme and obnoxious.

Displacement

A second ego defence mechanism is called 'displacement'. It usually refers to the indirect expression of an impulse that the censoring conscience (Freud's **super-ego**) prohibits us from expressing directly. For example, a child may develop a seething hostility towards his parents. Our social programming usually will not allow direct expression of this hostility. I mean, you can't hate your own parents. So, not in touch with the hostility which he had to repress, he smashes public property, overturns tombstones, or does something

It is socially fashionable to ask: Who am I? There is no little 'real self' inside of me. I am what I am committed to equally irrational. The apparent homicidal-minded boxing fan, who stands up at ringside and yells vociferously, 'Murder the bum!' as a helpless, senseless boxer is sinking to his knees, obviously harbours some subconscious hostility that has to be repressed because he can't live with it or express it.

'Scapegoating' is a common form of displacement. We react with uncalled for violence when someone looks at us in the wrong way, because there is a hostility in us that we cannot express directly. For some reason the person to whom we would like to express hostility seems too formidable to us. A man with a violent temper in the office may well be expressing the hostility he feels for his wife or for himself but cannot bring himself to express at home. Or the man who has been unjustly upbraided by his employer (of whom he is afraid because his job is at stake) may come home and take out his hostility on his wife and children. The prude, who cannot admit to her sexual nature directly, will take great interest in 'scandals' of a sexual nature. The lonely, isolated person, who cannot admit directly to his need for love and affection, will profess to be 'madly in love' with someone else (whom he does not really love at all).

A second meaning of 'displacement' is the device of disguising unpleasant realities to which we cannot admit (and therefore repress) by consciously stressing something else which is not so embarrassing to the ego. We profess to worry about some triviality to conceal some greater fear to which we cannot honestly admit. Or let us say that I am jealous of you, but I cannot really admit it, not even to myself. So I 'zero in' on some trivial annoyance, like the quality of your voice. I find it very grating. The husband and wife who have come to despise each other, but cannot openly admit to the real sources of their mutual agony, usually bicker about trivialities with great vehemence.

The man whose mother dominated his father is usually programmed to treat his own wife as an inferior. However, since he cannot admit to his resentment for his mother and her treatment of his father, or that he definitely wants his wife 'under' him, he will usually complain about small and inconsequential habits of hers. He will deny the value of her opinions and the wisdom of her actions. He will bitterly criticize her for the 'stupid way' she plays cards.

Projection

Another ego defence mechanism is called 'projection'. All of us tend to disown things in ourselves and to 'project' them into others. We try to rid ourselves of our own limitations by attributing them to someone else. Adam explained his sin to God by saying: 'The woman tempted me.' Eve ascribed the whole calamity to the serpent. It is also projection when we blame other things for our own failures, like the circumstances, the tools I had to work with, the position of the stars. We are tempted to ask the other fellow, 'Why don't you look where you're going?' when we bump into him.

It is a very common human inclination (projection) to dislike most in others what we cannot accept in ourselves. The real mystery of this projection is that we don't recognize these things in ourselves. They are repressed. We can strongly condemn in others what we cannot admit in ourselves. The stronger, the more exaggerated, the dislike of anything or any quality is manifested, the more it should be suspected as projection,

When someone gets a bug on 'hypocrisy', and often condemns it, and proclaims that it is widespread among the human race, it is most probable that he must repress all conscious recognition that he is himself hypocritical. The vain man, who can't admit to his own inclinations, suspects everybody of wanting attention and publicity. The ambitious person, who cannot honestly admit (and therefore represses) his own driving ambitions, usually feels that 'everybody is out for himself; all that most people want is fame and money.'

Then there's the paranoid (persecution complex victim) who projects his own self-hatred into others and feels that they don't like him. The prude thinks that every attractive man is making improper advances; she projects her own concealed (repressed) longing into every attractive male. A person with an uneasy conscience feels that others are suspicious of him, watching him. Very often, too, when someone puts his finger on a weakness in us, e.g. being too temperamental, we counter by charging: 'You're the one who is too temperamental!'

Introjection

'Introjection' is the ego defence by which we attribute to ourselves the good qualities of others. Introjection is prominent in what we call 'hero worship'. We identify with our heroes. Also, we identify our possessions with ourselves. We take great pride when someone praises our home, or we think that we are 'big time' because we come from a famous city, belong to a well-known fraternity, or

To understand people, I must
try to hear what they are
<u>not</u> saying, what they perhaps
will never be able to say.

have travelled to many places. Many women identify with the tragic heroines of soap-opera
programmes on television. A Manhattan psychiatrist
noticed that very many of his women patients had
relapses after becoming addicted to these shows.
They identified with all the unhappiness of the
suffering characters in these melodramas. This kind
of identification provides an easy access into a world
of fantasy and provides romance in our lives, though
sometimes the result of this ego defence is not very
profitable or consoling.

Rationalization

The most common form of ego defence is 'rationalization'. As a technique for self-justification, it is
hard to beat. We find some reason for our action
which justifies it. We 'think' (rationalize) our way to
a pre-ordained conclusion. Very often there are two
reasons for every thing we do: the alleged good
reason and the real reason. Rationalization is not
only self-deceit but eventually corrupts all sense of
integrity (wholeness). We rationalize our failures;
we find justification for our actions; we reconcile
our ideals and our deeds; we make our emotional

preferences our rational conclusions. I say that I drink beer because it has malt in it. The real reason is that I like it; it helps me feel uninhibited and secure with others.

As with all ego defence mechanisms, there is always something which I cannot admit in myself, something that I would like to do which appears wrong, or something that would make me feel better if I could believe it. Rationalization is the bridge which makes my wishes the facts. It is the use of intelligence to deny the truth; it makes us dishonest with ourselves, and, if we cannot be honest with ourselves, we certainly cannot be honest with anyone else. It consequently sabotages all human authenticity. It disintegrates and fragments the personality.

Insincerity, as an interior state of mind, is a psychological impossibility. I can't tell myself that I do and don't believe something at the same time. Choosing evil as evil is also a psychological impossibility, because the will can only choose the good. Consequently, to deny the truth I can't admit, and to do the deed which I cannot approve, I must necessarily rationalize until the truth is no longer true and evil becomes good.

Did you ever ask yourself the surprisingly difficult question: How does one choose evil? How do we commit sin? The will can choose, by its very nature, only that which is good. I am personally convinced that the exercise or use of free will in a given situation of guilt is that the will, desirous of some evil which has good aspects (if I steal your money, I will be rich), forces the intellect to concentrate on the good to be acquired in the evil act, and to turn away from the recognition of evil. This urges the intellect to rationalize that which was originally recognized as evil. While I am doing something wrong (in the act of doing it), I cannot be squarely facing its evil aspect; I must be thinking of it as good and right. Consequently, free will is probably exercised in the act of coercing the intellect to rationalize rather than in the execution of the act itself.

Caution: Human beings

In all of these ego defence mechanisms, please note that there is something that the person who operates the mechanism has felt the necessity of repressing. He cannot live with some realization. In one way or another, he keeps his psychological pieces intact by some form of self-deception. He just couldn't live comfortably with the truth, so he repressed it.

Therefore, and this is extremely important, the vocation of putting people straight, of tearing off their masks, of forcing them to face the repressed truth, is a highly dangerous and destructive calling. Eric Berne warns against disillusioning people about their 'games'. It may be that they just can't take it. They sought out some role, began playing some game, took to wearing some mask, precisely because this would make life livable and tolerable.

So we must be very careful, extremely careful in fact, that we do not assume the vocation of acquainting others with their delusions. We are all tempted to unmask others, to smash their defences, to leave them naked and blinking in the light of the illumination provided by our exposé. It could be tragic in its results. If the psychological pieces come unglued, who will pick them up and put poor Humpty Dumpty Human Being together again? Will you? Can you?

The greatest kindness: The truth

All that has been said in these pages would urge

us to be open and truthful about ourselves, our thoughts and emotions. It has urged us to be honest with ourselves and with others. Nothing is taken back here. But it is absolutely necessary to realize that nothing in these pages asks me or justifies me in becoming a judge of others. I can tell you who I am, report my emotions to you with candour and honesty, and this is the greatest kindness I can extend to myself and to you. Even if my thoughts and emotions are not pleasing to you, it remains the greatest kindness to reveal myself openly and honestly. Insofar as I am able, I will try to be honest with myself and communicate myself honestly to you.

It is another thing to set myself up as judge of your delusions. This is playing God. I must not try to be the guarantor of your integrity and honesty: that is your work. I can only hope that my honesty with and about myself will empower you to be honest with and about yourself. If I can face and tell you my faults and vanities, my hostilities and fears, my secrets and my shames, perhaps you will be able to admit to your own and confide them to me, if you wish.

It is a two-way street. If you will be honest with me, report your triumphs and tragedies, agonies and ecstasies to me, it will help me to face my own, and to become an integral person. I need your openness and honesty; you need mine. Will you help me? I promise that I will try to help you. I will try to tell you who I really am.

It costs so much to be a full human being that there are very few who have the enlightenment or the courage, to pay the price . . . One has to abandon altogether the search for security and reach out to the risk of living with both arms. One has to embrace the world like a lover. One has to accept pain as a condition of existence. One has to court doubt and darkness as the cost of knowing. One needs a will stubborn in conflict, but apt always to total acceptance of every consequence of living and dying.

Morris L. West
in The Shoes of the Fisherman

No one else can decide how
you are going to act . . .
Everyone must march to
his own drums.

6

A Catalogue of Games and Roles

There is no logical order in this partial listing of the roles and games which are very common patterns in human relations. Nor is there any restriction as to sex or age. Anyone can play one or more of these games. The ones you and I become proficient at or employ most often will depend upon our 'programming' and needs.

These games have one thing in common, no matter how different they may seem; they mask and distort the truth about the one most important thing that I could share with you: myself. I must ask myself: Which of these games do I play? What am I seeking? What am I hiding? What am I trying to win?

Always right

This person rarely, if ever, loses an argument. Even when the evidence begins to stack up against him, he can salvage respect for his position. He does not listen well and gives the appearance of expecting to learn little if anything from others. Basically, his self-esteem is threatened. His dogmatism is what Freud called 'reaction formation'. He acts doubly certain in order to guard against demoralizing doubts which stir in his subconscious and tend to undermine his certainty. His behaviour indicates the opposite of what seems to be true. He has deep, if subconscious, doubts about himself and his opinions.

All heart

Reaction formation is thought to be responsible for the excessively tender and sentimental concern of this person too. It is a subconscious compensation for his sadistic (cruel) tendencies. We all have cruel inclinations at times, but this person is particularly horrified by his.

The one thing about compensation is that, once it

is set in motion, it nearly always results in over-compensation. Somehow his programming has rendered him unable to be in touch with himself, to admit to hostile inclinations, and he spends most of his energy denying the truth he cannot admit. This person is likely to be excessively tender to pets (Mummy's little darling), gushing over children, over-indulgent with them, excessively demonstrative in showing affection and tenderness.

He follows his heart in all matters, to the point that others wonder if the head is operative at all. The heart decides everything. He can show all kinds of soft emotions, but will rarely if ever report harsher emotions precisely because he is afraid of these and must keep them repressed. Women are more inclined to this 'reaction formation' because our society programmes them to believe that hostile or cruel emotions are particularly horrifying in a woman.

Body beautiful, the

Usually physical vanity is a compensation for a gnawing sense of inferiority as a person. The beautiful or handsome person who plays this game, keeps staring into the mirror on the wall and into the mirror of the eyes of others (or in any shiny surface) for his own reflection, because he cannot find any deeper consolation. There is a sadness that hangs over vanity of this sort. Life is obviously over at 35. In the extreme, this person identifies his person with his body. He would answer the question, 'What are you?' with the response, 'I'm good looking.' And if he could be honest and open, he would add '. . . nothing more, just good-looking.'

Braggart, the

The game is a childish attempt to assert one's superiority. It is of the various manifestations of arrested emotional development. The braggart is usually a bully, too, if the situation allows. He wants to dominate others, either by words or, if he feels sure of himself, by physical strength. The indication is lack of self-esteem. He wants to feel important and discovers nothing in himself that satisfies this need. We sometimes ask him: 'Are you trying to convince us or yourself?' The answer is: both.

Clown, the

The compulsive clown is, like most of us, seeking some sort of recognition and attention. The sadness is that he thinks he can gain notice only by playing the fool for others. Deeper than this, it may be that he identifies with his act and tries to evade reality by taking nothing seriously. Clowning is sometimes an escape device. The clown doesn't know how to handle himself in a serious situation or how to react to sorrow, so he adopts an attitude of irresponsible gaiety. In dealing with others, his clowning serves as an adequate defensive mask (like the mask of the circus clown) to prevent others from knowing who he really is. He would rather laugh and joke than face the grim realities of life. He would rather put his act on the stage than lay his person on the line.

Competitor, the

In America, our culture has programmed most of us to accept competition as a part of the divine plan. The competitor must win whatever he does. He makes everything a 'win-lose' situation. He doesn't discuss; he debates. The triumphs that he seeks, so

The games we play
always follow
the programme

often at the expense of others ('Nice guys finish last!'), may be the outgrowth of emotional deprivation or lack of approval in his early life. The resultant insecurity causes him to question his worth, and he is consistently trying to prove this worth in competition and rivalry. His need for recognition intensifies the drive to 'get ahead'. He feels hostility towards anyone he feels is standing in his way or surpassing him. Sooner or later, he will be overcome by a sense of failure since the appetite for victory becomes increasingly voracious. He has, in the end, failed to prove his superiority and ends up in frustration. Basically, the problem is that he cannot distinguish between himself as a person and his accomplishment, between being and having. (See 'Inferior'   below.)

Conformist, the

This game is called 'peace at any price', and the price is surrender of all individuality to others. It usually begins with domineering authority and guilt feelings. The conformist won't or can't risk the acceptance of others. He is often praised for his willingness to 'go along', but he pays a high price in repressed emotions for the pittances of praise which he receives. His unwillingness to disagree with the established or fashionable opinion renders him an anonymity to others. He usually develops some sort of psychosomatic symptoms because his subconscious mind eventually becomes overloaded with all that he has had to repress in order to be 'the good guy who goes along with anything.' (See 'Guilty' below.)

Crank, the

The neurotic tendency which characterizes the crank is a low frustration tolerance. He doesn't do very well in situations of strain and stress. Usually the programming of the crank, like that of the competitor, involves early emotional deprivation, resulting in feelings of hostility. He feels deprived of personal security. He feels less sure of himself when things go wrong and nurses a long list of pet peeves, which he publishes for others from time to time. Those in his vicinity know that any one of these can send him into orbit, and this is the game aspect. Others are warned in various ways that they must not frustrate him.

Cynic, the

The excessive expectations of life often collapse and result in the cynic game. The person who is programmed to think that the universe should be tailored to his comfort often suffers a painful collision with reality. At this point, he strikes back with his cynicism. Basically, the cynic is a demoralized unrealist. Things have failed to turn out the way he wanted them, and so he takes his pains of disillusion out on everyone. You can't trust anyone. The whole system is corrupt. As long as he persists in his role as cynic, he won't have to take an honest look at himself and his world nor go through the pains of adjustment to reality. His facile wit is usually a symptom of submerged antagonism; he has not found life as he wanted it. He has never learned empathy or tolerance, and he has never experienced true affection for others. Consequently, he is a very lonely person behind his 'smirk'.

Deluded by grandeur

The game grows out of a mistaken sense of personal importance. The player has been programmed to portray to others a sense of importance. He is a name-dropper and tends to be 'I-centred' in conversation. Like the braggart, this person plays a game of compensation for inadequate self-esteem. There is always some effort to protect the ego from humiliation. He is attracted to dramatic deeds, a grandstander. He resents insignificance. He usually dreams about some magnificent memento by which the world will remember him when he is gone. The delusional system tries to afford him a sense of importance denied in reality. Obviously, it is difficult to be honest with him about himself.

Dominator, the

This game is characterized by an exaggerated desire to control the lives of others as well as their thought processes. Like most people who exaggerate their importance or wisdom, the dominator is bothered by subconscious feelings of inadequacy. It is strange that very often such a person is so determined to feel adequate that he is distracted from the factof his domineering ways. He usually explains his domination as necessary, reasonable and justifiable. The dominator is very often troubled by feelings of hostility. As he represses these, they find expression in selfishness and thoughtlessness in dealing with those he is supposed to love.

Dreamer, the

The game is clearly an 'escape' game. The dreamer is intent upon flight from reality. He achieves great things in his fantasy world, where he receives recognition and honours. Very often his dreams are a substitute for achievement and represent some kind of compensation for his lack of success with and in the real world. The dreamer usually likes movies and stories because they stoke his imagination with new settings and materials for future reveries. Eventually, he creates a comfortable world in which he can become 'somebody'. Very often the dreamer has ambitioned more than his abilities could reach, and he has to compensate himself in fantasy for his disappointment in reality. This is called 'neurotic fiction'. He has an alibi to explain every actual failure. He can't bring his ambitions into line with his abilities. What he needs most is courage to accept himself as he is.

Drinker, the problem
Dope addict, the

The dreamer escapes from reality on the magic rug of his fantasy; the drinker tries the route of narcosis. Those who are most vulnerable to stress are actually most in need of an escape. Addiction to drink or pot, etc., is usually found in those who react poorly to deprivation, who are most easily overcome by defeat, and who are most self-conscious and ill at ease with others.

The momentary release and experience of freedom, enjoyed under the sedation of excessive drink or dope, is usually followed by heightened anxiety and deeper depression when the haze clears. This, of course, brings on further need of sedation to deaden anxiety, the sense of guilt, and depression. Drinking and dope as a 'way out' are definitely limited in their capacity to do the job. Leaving reality, while the narcosis lasts, only makes it more difficult to return to reality and to live with it. The name of the game is a 'crutch' for sociability, self-expression, the concealment of embarrassment, and the possibility of forgetting one's troubles.

It is a law of human life,
as certain as gravity:
to live fully, we must
learn to <u>use</u> things
and <u>love</u> people . . .
not <u>love</u> things and
<u>use</u> people

Flirt, the

The 'flirting game' is basically an attempt to gain for the ego some kind of recognition. It is usually played by those who have never cultivated any real emotional depth. Only deeper relationships can result in security for the ego. They effect this security by promoting better self-knowledge and self-acceptance. The 'flirt' refuses to take the gamble of these more self-revealing relationships; he keeps running.

Flirting is possible only when the emotions are trivial and superficial, though none of us wants to admit this about his emotions. Stable and deeper human relationships can never be built in such emotions as the flirt possesses. The flirting game also assumes that when one tires of one conquest, he can move on to another. This is a rather selfish kind of sport, in which there are many injuries. No one wants to admit to being a flirt (or to playing any one of these games), but it is the first step to real emotional growth when we admit the tendency in order to hold it in some kind of check.

In all of these games, we must ask ourselves what it is that we really want, why we want it (which will always tell us something about ourselves), and why it would be better to give up our game. While flirting can bring some passing gratification to the ego, little passing infatuations often complicate life considerably, lead us into subterfuges, the invention of excuses, deceits, and preoccupation with self. Sexual and emotional development starts with narcissism (self-love) in the child, but with growth as a person, one should become more and more capable of altruism (love of another). The flirt has been somehow fixated in an adolescent state, and this growth has been arrested.

Fragile. Handle with care.

The 'fragile' person gives many advance signals to others that he is delicate and needs to be handled with great caution. Others are reluctant to confront the person with ready tear ducts and capable of instant-depressions, to deliver bad news, to ask him to accept responsibility (it is much easier to take it on yourself than ask him), or to offer him honest criticism. Fundamentally, this game grows out of a neurotic feeling of inability to cope with life. The fragility player exhibits a great sensitivity, too, to the estimate of others. His ego is tender; remarks or gestures are often misinterpreted. The fragile person is hyper-sensitive precisely because he places very little value on himself. This will usually not be clear to himself or others.

Fragility represents a regression to childhood, to a state of need and helplessness. If the game is played successfully, the person will never have to grow up or face the blood, sweat and tears of real life. The fragile person expresses with his sudden tears and traumas what the child is saying with his kicking and screaming. The demand is for the preferential treatment children so often require.

Gossip, the

The participant in the gossip-game, like most game-players, is in there for sensitive personal stakes. Unable to make the full use of his own abilities and being a defeatist at heart, and sorry for himself because he cannot measure up to his own ego ideal, he chooses to elevate his own self-esteem by undermining the esteem of others. Adler calls it the 'derogatory critique'. It is much easier to tear down others than lift oneself up by achievement. Superiority and inferiority being relative terms, lowering others seems to raise one's own status.

Benjamin Franklin once said that, if you want to know someone's faults, praise him to his peers. Gossiping can also be a salve for sensitive guilt feelings. We like to recite the misdeeds of others so we won't have to feel so badly about our own misdeeds. This accounts for our eagerness to learn the latest scandals from newspapers, magazines, etc., which readily oblige. After reading about vicious murders, etc., our own sarcasm and anger do not seem to be such terrible evils. Gain of the game: elevation of self and greater ease in living with one's regrets.

Hedonist, the

The 'my pleasure before all' type person tries to hide his emotional immaturity under various euphemisms ('just for "kicks!"'), but the immaturity surfaces quickly in the relationships. It is characteristic of the child and the neurotic (the emotional child) that he must have his pleasure and have it immediately. He will not inhibit for long any impulse to indulge himself. He is not able to suspend his grasping for pleasure even long enough to look at the implications of his actions.

The inability to postpone pleasure eventually

leads such a person to seek his pleasure in all things, at anyone's expense. When the stimulus of pleasure-to-be-had is registered, the response is automatic. Habits of hedonism are very often acquired as compensatory for the difficult aspects of life. 'I was overlooked or misunderstood, so now I can overeat or masturbate.' (Such logic is almost never examined consciously.)

I ... I ... I

It is almost a universal law that the extent of egocentrism in any person is proportionate to the amount of pain in him. It is a question of attention. One cannot give a great deal of attention to himself and to others simultaneously. We have only a limited amount of attention which we can confer. The destructive or diminishing part of pain is that it magnetizes attention to ourselves and to the area of our pain. Those who are suffering anything from a toothache to the loneliness of old age tend to egocentrism. Preoccupation with self often evolves into hypochondria (over-concern with health) or paranoia (persecution complex).

One cannor fashion himself to be the centre of the

universe and be content that others do not accept him as such. Whatever pains our past programming have left in us (guilt, inferiority, anxiety, etc.), these pains will inevitably led us into all the pitfalls of egocentrism. The egocentric does not mind what the contents of the conversation are about as along as they are about him. Eventually, he will fall into emotional depression because living in such a restricted world is living in a prison. He will suffer even more than the others who must live or work with him.

Inferior and guilty

Non-identical twins. Psychoanalytic literature distinguishes between inferiority feelings and guilt feelings, though both are manifestations of conflict between the actual self and the ideal self, between what one actually is and what one would like to be, between what one actually does or feels and what he thinks he should do or feel. The fundamental difference is that, in **inferiority** feelings, there is a recognition of weakness and inadequacy. People who suffer from inferiority feelings usually provoke competition and aggression. They seek to eradicate their feelings of inferiority by showing superiority in some form of rivalry. **Guilt** feelings on the contrary, can be verbalized: 'I am not much good. Most of what I want to do (my desires) and have done (my deeds) seem mean and evil. I really deserve contempt and punishment for my failures.' Guilt feelings inhibit the competitive spirit. They are reactions rather to hostile and aggressive impulses which one feels within himself.

To get rid of such guilt feelings, one usually tries to renounce the competition while inferiority feelings usually invite us to a competitive attitude. Guilt feelings usually persuade us to subordination; they usually surface in self-depreciation and even self-punishment. People generally try to free themselves from inferiority feelings by ambition and competition, by trying to get revenge or the upper hand. The extrication from guilt feelings is usually attempted through submission and the avoidance of any hostile or aggressive behaviour. Inferiority feelings tend to produce **rebels**; guilt feelings tend to produce **conformists** with modest and submissive ways.

Ambition and competition remain restricted to the imagination and the phantasy-life of the guilt-ridden person. He is usually a retiring, non-conspicuous type, who assiduously avoids contradictions.

He has a tendency to minimize his own abilities. After behaviour which his conscience cannot approve, the person with guilt feelings usually resolves that he will never again do the same thing. The person with inferiority feelings more often reacts by asking: 'Why not? Why not do these things? I'm not going to give into external or interior pressures on my conduct!' (See Franz Alexander, *Fundamentals of Psychoanalysys*, 1964).

Indecisive and uncertain

It has been said that the greatest misunderstanding a man can make is to be afraid of making mistakes. Indecision and uncertainty are ways of avoiding mistakes and responsibility. If no decision is made nothing can go wrong. The inclination to avoid decisions is sometimes manifested by dragging out as long as possible the ones we actually must make. The only real mistake is not learning from our mistakes.

The basic problem here is self-esteem and the protection of self-esteem. People who are indecisive fear that they will lose respect if their decision turns out to be wrong. Only little men, someone has said, are never wrong. We learn more from our mistakes than from our successes. But the indecisive person is so focused on his own ego and personal value that he does not see the validity of all these truths. The name of the game is safety and self-protection; the motto: Nothing attempted, nothing lost.

Very often, too, indecisiveness results in people who have been programmed by multitudinous (and sometimes contradictory) instructions and moralizing, or who have been reproached and embarassed for past mistakes. Finally, indecisiveness can result in a person's attempting to support more emotionally burdening problems than he can solve. He usually becomes rattled and can decide none of them.

Inflammable, handle with caution

It is hard for most of us to believe this, but people who have 'short fuses' and give forth loud noises are frequently reacting to some supposed grievance which is not that which really bothers them. As they cannot discuss openly the real grievance, they are letting off steam and their anger can rarely be taken at face value. What is smouldering in their subconscious is hostility. People are usually far more hostile towards each other than they realize (it is repressed), because our society has conditioned us to believe that hostility is unbecoming in socialized, civilized human beings.

Karl Menninger, in *Love Against Hate*, describes the chain reaction of parents with hidden hostilities frustrating their children and building up in them more repressed hostilities. Then the children grow up into frustrated parents who in turn frustrate themselves and their children. More hostilities! The first step in breaking this chain reaction, Menninger submits, is **to recognize the sources and extent of our aggression and hostility**, of which we are often unconscious. They are hidden (repressed) because people lead us to feel that we can't be angry (especially at our own parents, who have 'done so much' for us). Then we must neutralize these recognized hostilities by deepening our understanding or by releasing them in non-destructive ways (athletic competition). We are often most inflammable with those we love because it is usually against them that we bear the most hostility, since our dealings with them have been longer and more intense.

Intellect, the alias the egghead

Our social programming makes it much easier for us to be intellectual and to scorn fuller human reactions, especially insofar as they are emotional. Usually, the role of the 'intellect' is assumed by someone who is afraid of his emotions or is uncomfortable with them for one reason or another. Perhaps he was programmed not to show them, to think that sentiment was weakness. Sometimes, too, a person finds himself unable to relate easily with others, to enjoy friendship, and so he resorts to his pose of intellectualism.

The ivory tower of such intellectuals is also a common refuge from the competition involved in human relations. In themselves the learning processess are not threatening to most of us as are other people. The classroom is preferable to the cold, cruel world we have been taught to fear; more timid souls would rather read about life than try to live. Library stacks can be a retreat from the headaches of daily living, and they can provide the solace of isolation and the prestige of being a scholar. They can be an escape from social responsibilities.

People programmed for isolation are usually more inclined to scholarly work than to meaningful relations with others. Rather than admit that he is a hermit, shut off from society, the player of this game insists that he is dedicated to higher learning. Incidentally, this game frees us from social responsibilities, organizations, committees, paying dues and making friends. (Please note: This is definitely not intended as an indictment of scholars. The true scholar makes a valuable contribution to society, but no man is called to be a scholar at the expense of being a truly human being, a fully functioning person).

Loner, the

There is another escape pattern or game, which is very much like the ivory tower of intellectualism described above; it is the isolation game: the loner shuts himself off from others, lives alone, and tries to convince himself that he likes it this way. By entering this kind of solitary confinement, he succeeds in evading all the most difficult challenges of human life and society. He assumes the attitude of smugness; he smirks at organizations, laughs at the poor 'joiners', whom he looks upon with a pretended attitude of superiority and condescension. He keeps telling himself that he is superior to this sort of nonsense.

The neurotic is torn between his inner push towards and pull from people. The loner is a neurotic who opts in favour of the pulling away from people. He retreats, and, since he cannot relate easily to others, he plays his game to avoid failures in human relationships. The ultimate effects are conditioned by what is inside of the loner, the reasons for his withdrawal tendencies. If it is hostility that is predominant, it could eventually erupt into violence, as with Lee Harvey Oswald. If it is anxiety, it could result in compulsive-obsessive neurotic habits (e.g. repeatedly washing hands). If it is paranoia, it will deepen the gulf between himself and the rest of the human race. The escapist pattern always ends in some kind of tragedy.

Martyr, the

The persecution complex (paranoia) of 'the Martyr' is an emotional disorder characterized by many false suspicious beliefs. Paranoid trends are observed in one kind of schizophrenia, a mental disorder in which the sick person is separated from reality. In the neurotic paranoiac the outstanding characteristic is suspicion. He suffers from what psychologists call 'delusions of reference', which convince the paranoid that everyone is talking about him, that it rains on the day of his parade because God is holding something against him personally, etc. It is a feeling of being abused.

It should be said that something of this feeling is in all of us at times; very normal people at times suffer from delusions. In the normal person, however, these delusions are not so irrational, so extreme, or so crippling. The paranoiac often finds himself in the same predicament as the liar, who must invent stories to justify his misrepresentation of the facts. Eventually these delusions become systematized, and the individual tends to hang on to them in spite of all the apparent inconsistencies.

The persecutory delusions usually grow out of an inferiority complex. The individual hates his own inadequacy and projects his thinking into the minds of others; he concludes that they hate him too. He cannot establish satisfactory relationships with others and is generally oversensitive. His ego is very tender. In feeling rejected by others, he gradually withdraws into himself and becomes increasingly estranged and alienated from them. Then he is unable to check his imagined interpretations of the facts that he is misjudging. He feels that he was not suspicious enough of others, and they took advantage of him. Now he is too suspicious and feels that he cannot trust anyone.

Normal social relations are impossible to sustain with such an attitude of mind. All of us are somewhat suspicious. The opposite of this normal awareness would be gullibility or naïvety. The paranoiac has gone much too far. Paranoids implement their game by blaming other people for their mistakes. This habit, called 'passing the buck', is a normal part of the paranoid delusion. The paranoiac cannot evaluate properly his own responsibility as distinguishable from the role of others in causing his problems. His own self-deceptions seem absolutely clear and true to him.

The martyr complex grows out of an unstable self-evaluation and a failure to maintain a satisfactory degree of faith in others. Its expression is to blame others for our unhappiness. The paranoid is also aware of his own hostile feelings, but rationalizes them with his delusions. His desire is to attack others because he feels persecuted. Delusions in this way are simply attempts to create an imaginary situation in which the symptoms experienced within can appear rational and acceptable. The paranoid's capacity for rationalization is often remarkable, and sometimes he succeeds in convincing others of the rationality of his behaviour.

Messiah, the

This game calls for a little imagination (and a subconscious need to feel important). The Messiah fancies himself saviour of the human race. It could well be a reaction-formation to the fear of insignificance. He thinks of himself as the 'helper' and others as the 'helped' in almost all of his relationships. Instead of urging others to use their own strength and wisdom, he dutifully lends out his. If he looks around his life, he will discover that he relates to very few people as equals. If people are attracted to know him because of his good qualities which are not completely submerged by his assumed role, it will be better for them to have a problem or need.

The gain of the game is a rather large, expansive feeling and a long, well-memorized list of those whom he has helped. Basically, the Messiah has inferiority feelings and seeks to free himself from these by dominating others emotionally.

Mummy, the

The overprotective mother plays a very harmful game. Mummies usually produce little monsters, utterly selfish people who demand their own way in everything. Mummy's child is tragically unprepared for a world which is totally unprepared to baby him and accede to his every whim. Psychological studies done on soldiers in wartime show that those who 'crack up' most often and most severely are the products of over-protective mothers. The most often requested song of soliders, when Bing Crosby visited the South Pacific troops in World War II, was Brahm's 'Lullaby'.

This game is not motivated by a genuine, healthy and mature love. There are three possible causes: (1) *Neurotic anxiety*. The insecure mother is fearful that her child may suffer some harm unless she does everything for him. This fear is usually transmitted to her children. Such a mother does not enjoy her children and only worries about them. (2) *Hostility*. Strange as this may seem, maternal overprotection is sometimes an over-compensation (reaction-formation) for a subconscious hostility towards her children. She atones for her personal dislike of her children by conscientious devotion to them.

(3) *Frustrated marital relations*. The mother who is unhappy with her husband frequently pours her pent up feelings of affection on her child. Under such circumstances the child bears the brunt of the unsatisfied love-life of the mother. (See David Levy, *Maternal Overprotection*, Columbia University Press.)

Peace at any price

(See **Inferior and Guilty**)

Ponce de leon

This is the game of the person who is ageing and simply cannot adjust to the fact. Frequently, middle-aged people feel that they are losing their attractiveness. Baldness, the middle-age spread, wrinkles around the neck, symbolize declining prestige among the opposite sex. To compensate for this deterioration of age, those who have never developed as true persons and who have never developed deeper emotional ties with others usually begin looking for a young lover. In addition to the physical evidence, which shows in the mirror, these people also compensate for an emotional 'slump', which is

When I repress my
emotions, my stomach
keeps score . . .

evidenced in loss of ambition, fatigue and more frequent fits of depression. Biologically, this can be due to insufficient hormone production.

The tragedy of this game is that these people have suffered emotional arrest and have never learned to relate meaningfully as persons; they have very little left for consolation in middle age. They have prized their 'sex appeal' and fear that it is waning. Sadly, they try to hide their double chins, varicose veins, the wrinkles, grey hair, etc., by trying to think and act young. Sex appeal has never and could never be the key to the finer things in life, that can sustain the ageing.

Poor mouth, the

This game is played by those who appear to be self-depreciating. The player talks himself down, perhaps in search of reassurances which assuage his 'guilt feelings' (See also **Inferior and Guilty**.)

Pouter, the

The pouting game is played by emotional children. The pouter cannot sit down and openly discuss interpersonal problems, usually because his position or grievance is irrational and he secretly knows it. He can scourge others emotionally by his silence, sad looks, etc., without having to tell them what is bothering him. He can sulk without accepting the responsibility of having to explain why he is acting this way. An explanation might sound so silly that he knows (peripherally) that the other person might laugh; he can derive his needed satisfaction and indulge his own self-pity without having to work out difficult situations through communication. (See also **Fragile. Handle with care.**)

Prejudice and bigotry

This game is the outgrowth of a social neurosis which flourishes chiefly among the insecure. The prejudiced person needs some kind of vent for his emotional hostilities. The scapegoat in this situation will certainly not be helped in his own development if he is abused in this way. Gordon Allport, in *The Nature of Prejudice*, suggests that prejudice arises from our anxieties; we feel insecure, and so we form around us an in-group as a kind of buffer of protection. Those outside of my 'in-group' are thought to be a threat and menace. I lash out at them because I am somehow threatened by them. I cannot logically suggest why (though many reasons are adduced), but anyone who is not in my in-group is necessarily a threat to me if I am highly anxious and insecure.

Prejudice is an emotional delusion, but, wherever it exists, it is never recognized as such by those who are prejudiced by it. The bigot will inevitably try to explain his prejudice (pre-judgement equals judgements prior to consideration of evidence) in intellectual terms. He could hardly admit the irrationality of his position.

Society very often helps us with the work of the rationalization needed to explain our prejudices; most bigots therefore don't have to work out their own rationalized, logical explanation. They can just recite well-rehearsed lines.

Procrastinator, the

The 'mañana' game attempts to evade reality by postponing the things that should be done, that should be done here and now. The procrastinator has to deceive himself by unrealistic assurances, like, 'I'll cut down on my smoking as soon as I can go on a vacation.' 'I'll start exercising when the weather gets better.' 'I'll start going to church again when I settle down and have my own family and children.' Escaping into vague and unrealistic tomorrows is only one of the many varieties of evasion of reality commonly sought by men. (See **Indecisive and Uncertain**.)

Resentfully yours

When the born-loser type personality looks for a scapegoat for his own failure, he very often blames someone or something else: the Establishment, life, the breaks. He resents the success and happiness of others because his own life, by comparison, is unhappy. He has been somehow deprived. We are all tempted to make our own failures understand-able by explaining them in terms of something other than our own inadequacies. Unfair treatment by others, injustice, the conspiracy of circumstances, etc., make our failures look easier to face.

The resenter uses up all his energies resenting, and therefore usually accomplishes very little. Sometimes it seems that the most vicious critics of anything (national government, school, church, etc.) are very often the ones who do nothing for the institutions which they criticize so vocally. The resentful person is forever trying to bring his case before the court of life, hoping that the jury of others will acquit him of his failures.

Resentment comes from the Latin **resentire** (to feel all over again); the resenter is always rehashing the past, reliving past battles he cannot win, and he often persists in his game for a lifetime. Resentment becomes an emotional habit. No one's feelings are caused by others. Our feelings are caused by our own emotional response, our own choices and reactions. The resenter is a reactor, not an actor, and eventually, when he realizes this, he is left with no vestiges of self-respect. He has spent his life employing a failure mechanism, and he somehow knows it.

Sex-bomb and predatory male, the

Barring the sick condition of the nymphomaniac who is obsessed with sex, most girls who play the 'Sex Bomb' game do so not because they really enjoy genital sexuality or because they are 'highly sexed'. It is rather because they feel they have nothing else to offer but a provocative body. They want to gain male attention, and desire to be popular. The little ruse of this game usually pays off, but the emotion-

ally arrested males it attracts are always very regret-
table conquests. Besides this sad motive of reaching
out for affection and attention, sometimes the 'Sex
Bomb' is trying to reject her parents, to spite them.

'The Predatory Male' is usually an ego-hunter,
looking for some new trophy of conquest. His inferiority feelings (see **Inferior and Guilty**) are deep,
and he wants to compensate for them by trying to
make conquests of the opposite sex. Sometimes,
successful 'ladies' men' are merely neurotics who are
industriously engaged in an attempt to cover up
their personal insecurity. They are more to be pitied
than censored.

The sadness of both 'Sex Bomb' and 'Predatory
Male' is that they are seeking some kind of human
intimacy or nearness. Because personal closeness
takes a long time, and demands much honesty (gut-
level communication), and because these people
feel totally inadequate to pay this price of true
personal intimacy, they substitute physical intimacy.
They are not equipped, they feel, to do any better.
Nobody takes to the useless side of life, Alfred Adler
says, in his book *What Life Should Mean to You*,
unless he fears that he will be defeated if he remains
on the useful side. Those who play this game are
usually so emotionally undeveloped that the Don
Juan pattern claims them for life, and they are

unable to confer their love lastingly on anyone, if, indeed, they are capable of love at all.

Suffering is the spice (price) of life

Some neurotics have been so conditioned that they feel guilty for enjoying anything in life. As Abraham Lincoln once said, 'People are about as happy as they decide that they are going to be.' This masochistic game calls for renewed penance for every pleasure. This person rarely spends money on frivolous things; he does not really enjoy an evening if the price of admission is high. He tends to get involved in love-situations that are hopeless, and becomes infatuated by someone who is totally beyond his reach. If he does catch himself having a good time, he will devise, like a contrite sinner, some manner of punishing himself for it. Material gains seem futile and meaningless, and the sufferer rarely realizes that the deficiency is really inside himself.

Fundamentally, the problem is usually guilt feelings. These people don't think that they deserve to have pleasant thoughts or to enjoy good times. The person who is programmed for this game is usually afflicted also with scruples and tends to paranoia.

He punishes himself with scrupulosity and projects his self-hatred into others, believing that they must feel about him as he himself does. He is externalizing his own guilt feelings. His inner voices are converted into outer voices. Such a person is also very concerned to please others and dreads their disapproval. He is not able to relate deeply to many people, if any at all, because his basic self-hatred sabotages all his relationships.

Strong, silent type, the v. willing and wordy

There are two ways to keep from communicating yourself to others, and, because of various fears, most of us are reluctant to let others know who we really are. Two very effective techniques to prevent communication are (1) to say very little. People may think that you are profound if you don't open your mouth. An old saw says that 'deep rivers run quietly'. The other way is (2) to say so much that they can't possibly sort it all out and figure out anything about you. You can't say a great deal, using this buckshot technique of obscurity, without giving a lot of contradictory indications. No one can possibly accuse you of not doing your part to communicate. Only the sharper members of the group will realize that they don't know what the devil you've been talking about.

Worrier, the

Rollo May, in his book, *The Meaning of Anxiety*, says that normal anxiety is proportioned to the objective threat or danger to the existence of an individual as a person. Neurotic anxiety is **disproportionate** to the objective danger. The most common cause of anxiety is the insecurity an individual has experienced as an infant and child. If the infant is not given the needed sensations of security, if he is not held in secure arms, rocked tenderly to sleep etc., and if the child is not sure of his parents' love, the level of anxiety will probably be high in this person. The game always follows the programme.

As a game, worry is an immature way to handle one's difficulties. The worrier usually gets on a treadmill, goes over the same ground again and again, getting nowhere. (In the end, however, he gets ulcers.) He repeats useless statements of his problem, rehearses alternatives without reaching any decision, and counts all the possible consequences of possible decisions again and again. The worrier would probably feel guilty for not doing anything constructive, so he does something: He worries. (Got a 'term paper' coming up?)

Psychologically, worry is related to anxiety, which results from super-charged **repressed emotions** (e.g. hostility) with or without any external threats. It is therefore possible for the chronic worrier to feel ill at ease without knowing what is actually bothering him. The internal pressures of repressed emotions do not always need external stimuli to produce this uncomfortable condition. It is one of the high prices we pay for emotional repression.

'Sorry, but that is the way I am . . . I was like this in the beginning, am now, and ever shall be . . .' is a handy motto and delusion to have around you if you don't want to grow up.